in the shadow
of the
masters

grandmaster Deng ke yu

By Bob Fermor

DISCLAIMER

The author(s) and publisher of this material are: **NOT RESPONSIBLE**
in any manner what so ever for any injury which may occur through
reading or following the instructions in this material.
The activities, physical and otherwise, described in this material may be
too strenuous or dangerous for some people, and the reader(s)
should consult a doctor before engaging in them.

ISBN: 0 954111 80 X

First published 2001

Published in the UK by:
N.A.M.A. Publications
Web site: www.nama.co.uk
E-mail: fon-moor-kuin@tinyworld.co.uk

CONTENTS

04:     Dedication

05:     What Others Have Said

13:     Foreword

19:     Introduction

24:     Requirements of the 85 Forms

33:     Far Ging - Exercises

39:     Traditional Warm Up Exercises of the Nine Points

58:     Traditional Yang 85 Forms

61:     Traditional Yang 85 Forms Section 1

80:     Yang Style Applications of Section 1

87:     Traditional Yang 85 Forms Section 2

136:    Yang Style Applications of Section 2

143:    Traditional Yang 85 Forms Section 3

208:    Yang Style Applications of Section 3

215:    Yang Style Single Hand TUI SAU (exercises)

225:    Yang Style Double Hand TUI SAU (exercises)

264:    Yang Style Walking Pushing Hands TUI SAU

274:    Conclusion

DEDICATION

I had no idea how difficult it would be to produce a book, but through the hard work and dedication of my students, the support of my wife Joanne Fermor and my three sons, Ben, Jordan and Brandon, this book has been made possible.

I would like to personally thank those who have been there right from the beginning. David Watts and Alistair Probert, for their enthusiasm and hard work, as without their help and dedication this book would not have been possible. Last of all a personal thank you to my good and long time friend Kevin Brewerton, for his loyalty and friendship.

I would like to dedicate this book to my mum Doris Fermor who is no longer with us, but will always be in my thoughts and to my good friend Tony Chan who has also sadly passed away at such a young age. Without his influence and inspiration of the Chinese martial arts I would never have met Master Deng Er Qian.

David Watts, Co-Author

Being a Web/Graphic Designer, I found that helping Bob to produce this book was at times very challenging but well worth the long hours and effort required to complete the project. I now fully understand why it takes a certain kind of person to write a book, but I can quite honestly say now that I have gained the experience. I am looking forward to helping Bob on the next book.

Bob with his good friend Tony Chan.

Bobs mum Doris Fermor.

WHAT OTHERS HAVE SAID

Martial arts have given me many things, world titles, a discipline and purpose in my life, and an art and code of ethics that I follow, to name a few. It has also given me a friendship with Bob.

We met many years ago as student/teacher, but that was only the beginning of what has grown into much more. We have travelled around the world together and shared the exhilaration of competition. I have fought in places like New York, where the battle was intense, and just before stepping out into the final round, I looked behind me and saw Bob there, yes he is a friend.

His path as a martial artist has always been complete, and his passion in weapons is what gave him a name and certain status that the general martial arts public have come to know him by, but it is his many years of studying and teaching the art of Tai Chi that has called upon him to travel to the roots in China (which he has done for many years), to trace the origins of his art and develop himself in a true way.

I now know that by deciding to write this book, will give martial artists everywhere (that follow the same path), an opportunity to learn from his knowledge and his great enthusiasm to teach. Seize the opportunity. I wish him the best and give him the full support as he has given me for many years.

Kevin Brewerton 5 times World Champion

James Sinclair on top of the mountains at Tai Wo, Hong Kong.

I first met Bob Fermor in 1987 when we were teaching on a multi-style seminar. At this time Bob was specialising in weaponry and demonstrated considerable talent in the use of single and double nunchaku. We met again the following year for a larger version of the seminar now aptly named 'Super Seminar'. We talked and realised that our paths would be crossing again in Hong Kong as we both were further researching our martial arts training.

Still at this time Bob was searching for his way and was not a 'formalised stylist' his pragmatic nature led him to speak his mind and upset the weaker souls around. We did meet up in Hong Kong and on one occasion there were a number of martial artists from different schools gathered having tea in the lobby of a Kowloon hotel. We were discussing the finer details of certain theories and principles despite our different styles. Bob became a little outspoken and ended up challenging me to a sparring session in the village of Tai Wo in the New Territories.

I turned up to find him training with the broad sword and ready for action. Bob was a W.A.K.O weapons champion and a great competition fighter. We then trained and Bob saw that traditional training can have its place and mutual respect was earned. Bob also has a wicked sense of humour and after a free hand practice he then challenged me to a fight with poles. I didn't think to travel by bus and train with an 8 foot pole!

Bob then pulled out a bamboo pole hidden behind a wall, we faced each other and got ready, as any mistake can be serious when dealing with weapons. He launched in and I managed to parry his pole down only to find my pole had broken in two and Bob was moving in for the kill laughing his head off. I still do not know to this day if he had set me up!

The next time I met Bob again was in 1999 in Los Angeles. We arranged to train on Venice beach. We had lost contact for a long time and it came to pass that Bob had been seriously involved in the study of Tai Chi and was looking for a link with Wing Chun's sticky hands and Tai Chi's pushing hands. We trained, and it was obvious that Bob was now a martial artist in the traditional sense but still with his ever-present gusto.

Bob is a genuine man who will not suffer fools gladly, and is dedicated to training and improving. He drives for more knowledge but not to simply have a wealth of information that is not used, Bob is concerned with ability and skill at all levels.

James Sinclair
Chief Instructor
U.K Wing Chun Association

James I am sorry about the pole.

(Photograph by Sylvio L. Dokov)

Although best renowned for his remarkable skill with the nunchaku, Bob Fermor has for many years now immersed himself in a serious study of the Chinese Martial Arts.

His book 'In the Shadow of the Masters' is a must read for any serious martial artist and one which I am sure will be appreciated by all.

Bob Sykes

Bob Fermor has travelled the world extensively meeting many important exponents of different styles of the martial arts. Bob has never been one to shy away in any conversation that would help him to further his knowledge. He will not tolerate fools or get into any discussion with any one who just talks about 'their' style. Bob firmly believes that actions speak louder than words.

Before studying Tai Chi, Bob and his wife Joanne entered many competitions and made many good friends along the way. Bob feels that if one is to make his mark, get noticed, or get credibility in the martial art world, then competition is the place to achieve this. This is what Bob and Joanne set out to do.

Bob and Joanne have been practicing martial arts for many years and have been noted for their exceptional skills in the use of weapons. They were very much in the public eye of the martial arts world between 1984 & 1995 when they were well renowned on the tournament circuit.

During this period they appeared regularly in magazines and could always be found performing demonstrations or competing in national and international competitions, winning many trophies and accolades along the way. Their abilities, attitude and commitment to their art has ensured their success.

Bob Sykes editor of M.A.I called him 'The Weapons Wizard'.
Kevin Brewerton called him 'The Gypsy Showman'.
Tim Ayling editor of Fighters named Bob & Joanne
                                    'The King and Queen of Kata'.

SUMMARY OF ACCOLADES

1984   Nunchaku de Combat, Paris, European Championships, 2nd place B. Fermor.

1986   B.N.A British Nunchaku Championships, 1st place B. Fermor, 1st place J. Fermor.

1986   European Black Belt Championships, Ireland, Weapons division, 1st place B. Fermor.

1986   Bob Fermor features on the front cover of Fighters Magazine.

1987   Ireland Kung Fu Championships, 1st place B. Fermor, 2nd place J. Fermor.

1987   A.K.F.A British Championships, 1st place B. Fermor, 2nd place J. Fermor.

1988   A.W.A Welsh Weapons Championships, 1st place B. Fermor, 1st place J. Fermor.

1988   B.N.A British Nunchaku Championships, 1st place B. Fermor, 1st place J. Fermor.

1988   National Demonstration Championships, Liverpool, 2nd place F.M.K Kung Fu.

1988   F.S.K Championships, Manchester, 2nd place B. Fermor.

1988   W.A.K.O. British Championships, 3rd place B. Fermor, also selected for the British team.

1989   F.S.K. Championships, Manchester, weapons, 1st place B. Fermor.

1989	F.S.K Championships Manchester, 1st place J. Fermor, Creative Kata.
1989	M.A.I. Nat. Championships Huddersfield, 1st place B. Fermor.
1989	M.A.I. Nat. Championships Hatfield, 2nd place B. Fermor.
1989	W.A.K.O. Nat. Championships Gold Medal, B. Fermor.
1989	M.A.I. Nat. Championships Liverpool, 2x 2nd place B. Fermor, 2nd place J. Fermor.
1989	National Demonstration Championships Liverpool, 1st place F.M.K.
1989	Bob Fermor features on front cover of M.A.I.
1990	W.A.K.O. Nat. Championships Gold Medal, B. Fermor.
1990	F.S.K. Nat. Championships Grand Champion, B. Fermor.
1990	F.S.K. Nat. Championships Grand Champion, J. Fermor.
1990	M.A.I. Nat. Championships Nottingham, 1st place B. Fermor, 2nd place J. Fermor.
1990	M.A.I. Nat. Championships Cheltenham, 1st place B. Fermor, 3rd place J. Fermor.
1990	M.A.I. Nat. Championships Huddersfield, 2nd place B. Fermor, 2nd place J. Fermor.
1990	MAI. Nat.Championships Grand Champion (forms) B. Fermor.
1990	Martial Arts Illustrated Magazine nominates Bob Fermor into the Black Belt Hall of Fame.
1990	W.A.K.O. World Championships Venice, Italy, Bronze Medal B. Fermor.
1990	Cambridgeshire Opens, 1st place B. Fermor.
1990	W.A.K.O. European Championships Madrid, Spain, Silver Medal B. Fermor.

1990   Demonstrations for the Lord Mayor, Sligo, Ireland.

1990   Battle of Westchester, New York, U.S.A. 3rd & 4th place B. Fermor.

1991   W.A.K.O. World Championships Crystal Palace, England 2x
        Bronze Medals J. Fermor, 4th place B. Fermor.

1991   W.A.K.O. National Championships Gold Medal B. Fermor.

1991   Battle of Westchester, New York, U.S.A. 3rd place B. Fermor.

1992   Bob & Joanne Fermor (Austin) features on the front cover of
        Fighters Magazine.

1993   Battle of the Region Farnham 2x 1st place B. Fermor.

1993   K.D.O.O.A. Fleet 2x 1st place J. Fermor.

1993   Ricochet Nat. Birmingham 3x 1st place B. Fermor, 2nd place
        J. Fermor.

1994   Ricochet Nat. Birmingham 1st place B. Fermor, 2nd place
        J.Fermor.

1994   Euro Classics 2nd & 3rd place B. Fermor.

1995   World Classics England 2x 1st place B. Fermor, 2nd place
        J.Fermor.

1995   Bob Fermor awarded a trophy
        for his dedication in martial arts
        by Kevin Brewerton 5 times
        World Champion.

Bob, Joanne and their son Jordan, with Kevin Brewerton and his daughter Kyla, in Hollywood Hills, California.

FOREWORD

Bob Fermor, Master Deng, Master Deng's pupil, David Watts and Mrs Deng (front).

I have been training in the martial arts since 1990. I first heard about Bob Fermor in January 1998 from a friend who was lodging at my house. When I heard the stories about this 3 times World Champion, renowned for his weapons skills and now practising Tai Chi close to where I was living, I felt I had to meet him. I obtained his phone number and called him up to ask if I could visit him, Bob was very open with me on the phone and invited me to visit his club.

I will always remember the night I first met Bob at his club, I was not disappointed, Bob took time out from his lesson to demonstrate his Kung Fu, Weapons and Tai Chi skills, he was very open about his knowledge and teaching methods and he told me about Master Deng in Shanghai. This first meeting blew my mind and I immediately asked if Bob would except me as a student, I have been training with him ever since and never looked back.

Since knowing Bob I have gained much respect for him, through his open teaching methods, knowledge and the lineage behind his knowledge. He never holds back from his students and his teachings are kept simplistic as they were traditionally taught to him by Master Deng. It seems rare these days in the western world to find a teacher like Bob who can explain their art in plain black and white terms without clouding the martial art with unnecessary complexities and even rarer to find a teacher who will so openly share their knowledge with their students.

I find it somewhat amazing that someone as renowned as Bob and with such high calibre lineage, that he is almost never invited to visit other practitioners clubs. I feel it is a shame that some people seem to be unwilling to accept Bob's honest nature, believing him to be too outspoken.

When Bob told me it was a dream of his to share the knowledge taught to him by Master Deng, by writing a book, I jumped at the opportunity to be involved in the project. Bobs vision was to author a Yang Style Tai Chi Chuan book encompassing the essence of Master Deng's teachings. The emphasis on the book should be a training manual and reference of the practical application of Yang Tai Chi for all serious martial artists.

During the research stages of the book another opportunity that I would have been stupid to turn down was offered to me by Bob, this time it was the chance

Shanghai Chin Woo Athletic Association - head quarters

to go to Shanghai in China to visit Master Deng. I considered myself incredibly lucky to have been asked and again jumped at the chance. Bob and I went out to Shanghai not knowing what to expect, but it was clear to me from the outset that Bob fully intended to get the most out of the trip and to make things happen. The trip was only one week long and I am still amazed how much Bob achieved in this short space of time.

On the first day in Shanghai Bob and I took a walk in the Botanical Gardens behind our hotel, it was early in the morning and we hoped to see Tai Chi being played. At first we could only find the Chinese jogging, walking backwards and doing slow exercises, but as we searched around we started to discover the areas of the park where all manner of Tai Chi and Chinese martial arts were being practiced, from Chen Style to Fan, but by far the most wide spread was Yang Style Tai Chi and it was the same as how Master Deng had shown Bob, who in turn had shown me.

Bob decided to start practicing his Yang 85 Forms, to see what would happen, at first we mainly got odd looks, we decided to carry on looking around the park, when we found a group practicing Yang Style and some others practicing Yang Straight Sword. Bob again started to perform, this time a couple of the more senior Chinese started to take more interest in what Bob was doing, this time smiling and gesturing as if happy to see such a high standard and also maybe a little surprised that a Westerner could do it. At this Bob gestured to borrow a sword to perform his sword form. Bob performed his Yang Style Broad Sword, a crowd of Chinese had started to gather around us to see what was happening. By the end of the form the senior Chinese man who had lent the sword to Bob was getting very excited. A couple of Chinese men walking past made a comment in English, at this Bob asked them if they understood English well and a conversation was struck up. By the end of this conversation they had invited us to go and meet Master Mao, who was renowned as the top teacher in the whole park and we later discovered was a top Bagua practitioner who had learnt from the Shaolin temple. The Chinese men took Bob and I out of the park and to the home of Master Mao. As we got to Master Mao's house, he turned up on his bicycle. The men spoke in mandarin to Master Mao, after which Bob started to demonstrate various forms to Master Mao, although Master Mao did not speak any English and Bob only knew a few words in Cantonese, the two exchanged a conversation through martial art moves. Afterwards the two Chinese men who could speak some English explained that if we met them in the park the next morning, Master Mao would start to teach us Dragon Style Bagua. Bob spent every morning learning part of the Bagua form and has since returned to Shanghai to learn the second half of the form.

A few days into our visit to Shanghai Bob and I visited Master Deng at his home. Master Deng was so happy to see Bob again and I got the opportunity to meet Master Deng and his family which for me was a great honour indeed and a moment in my life I will always cherish. A little while into our visit Master Deng asked his daughter to phone his top student in Shanghai. His student, on hearing Bob was visiting, decided to rush over to the house. While we were waiting Bob told me to demonstrate section one of the 85 forms. When I had finished, Master Deng just smiled and gave me a thumbs up sign. For me there could be no greater compliment, towards my Tai Chi development of the teachings of Master Deng as passed on to me by Bob, and it's a credit to Bobs teaching methods. Soon after this Master Deng's student arrived and immediately wanted to play Tui Sau pushing hands with Bob. They faced off in the living room and started to play, it was plain to see from the outset that Bob was taking control. They applied techniques and counters, Bob often landing a good technique and pushing his opponent away. You could see that Master Deng's student was getting frustrated and started to try and lean his whole body weight in towards Bob, but Bob remained in a strong posture, firmly rooted to the ground, while his opponent was slipping and being pushed. Throughout the encounter Master Deng watched intently and just smiled. Finally Bob decided to take his opponent out in style by sending him flying onto an empty sofa, at this point Master Deng just started to laugh, and this friendly encounter ended. Master Deng said how pleased he was and that he thought that Bob had moved on in the Yang Style. Later back at the hotel Bob told me he had never seen the master laugh so much.

While in Shanghai Bob wanted to make a point of visiting the world famous Chin Woo Athletic Associations HQ. With the help of Master Deng's daughter and her persistence, a meeting was eventually set up with the head of the Shanghai Chin Woo and the secretary. Bob, myself, Master Deng's daughter and a translator attended the meeting. After the initial introductions and exchange of business cards we were led to the Chin Woo meeting chamber, a beautifully decorated room with ornately carved chairs around the walls. At first our hosts seemed unsure as to what Bob wanted to achieve from the meeting and although they were very hospitable, they did not seem to be particularly interested. Through the aid of our translator, Bob started to explain how much he respected the Chinese for their martial art abilities and that he believed much of the top Tai Chi was played in Shanghai. Bob went on to explain that because of this legacy he felt it was vitally important that the Chin Woo should lead the world in the recognition and promotion of Tai Chi, including Tui Sau Pushing Hands in their syllabus. By now our hosts were starting to take more interest and were very pleased to see a foreigner taking such interest in the preservation of the traditional Chinese styles of martial arts, but they were still not fully convinced. It was at this point in the meeting when Bob said "please allow me to demonstrate" and gestured for me to join him in the centre of the meeting chamber. Bob and I both faced off in 'ward off' position and commenced to perform 'Grasp the Bird's Tail'. By now the Chin Woo attendees interest was increasing. Bob and I continued to demonstrate various techniques from the 37 postures of the 85 forms, always starting from and returning to 'Grasp the Bird's Tail'. After demonstrating various techniques we then showed the techniques in practice by playing traditional Tui Sau, where anything goes, through sensitivity we used 'feeling and listening energy' to intercept and find openings to apply our Tai Chi techniques. We applied various techniques in quick succession with counter upon counter until Bob caught me with a brilliant Brush Knee Push, which sent me sprawling into the lap of the head of the Chin Woo association. By now our hosts were laughing and clasping their hands with excitement. Bob and I returned to our seats, our hosts visibly impressed and surprised to see such a level of skill performed by two foreign visitors. The meeting now took on a new level of importance with further discussions. The meeting was concluded with Bob receiving a formal invitation to return to Shanghai for the official opening of the newly constructed Chin Woo HQ building. Bob has since been back to Shanghai for further visits to the Chin Woo HQ, training with some of the head coaches.

Bob always tells his students that "a book is not a teacher, only a reference" and this book is a brilliant reference, full of information for the practical martial artist who is studying Tai Chi and who would like to know that little bit more about the essence of Tai Chi as a formidable martial art.

I know this book will give you a taste of Master Deng Er Qian's vast knowledge as passed on to Bob Fermor and hopefully it will give you an idea of what it is like to train in the shadow of a master. So enjoy the book and what it has to offer.

David Watts
N.A.M.A Student

Bob Fermor, Master Mao and David Watts in the Botanical gardens, Shanghai, China

Bob Fermor walking the circle in Bagua

INTRODUCTION

Having trained in the martial arts for the past 25 years, Tai Chi has enabled me to continue my martial art career. It was in 1989 when I first started practicing Tai Chi in the shadow of my master, Deng Er Qian.

This chapter of my life began when a very good friend informed me that master Deng Er Qian from Shanghai was coming to England to visit his family. During this visit, my friend intended on doing some training with him and asked if I would like to come along and train with them. I was very pleased to be invited but personally I did not think that Tai Chi was for me. I had always hoped that my friend might teach me a style called 'Pak Mei' that he had learnt from his uncle who was very famous in the Chinese Community both in England and Hong Kong, but as my friend explained this was not possible as his uncle would only teach Chinese people and not western people. My friend insisted that I should meet Master Deng, he said "you should never judge a book by its cover, it is what's inside that counts".

I will never forget the day when my wife Joanne and myself went to meet Master Deng. At the time Joanne and I were well renowned on the tournament circuit in England, participating in the weapons division, winning many national and international titles along the way. Master Deng was in his late 70's, he was a very pleasant man who could not speak very much English. My friend approached him and started to speak with him in Mandarin. A big smile appeared on the master's face and they both turned around and looked at Joanne and myself. My friend said "Come on Bob, have a go with him". I thought this was a joke. I had just won two world titles in the forms category and he wanted me to fight a man in his late 70's.

Master Deng came towards me and held up his hand and said "okay". I looked across to Tony and asked "What does he want?" he replied "He wants to feel you, he wants to do Pushing Hands with you". I did not know what 'Pushing Hands' was. He could see I was confused and he said "Just let your hand touch his hand and push him". I could not believe I was going to do this, but over I went and both of our hands touched. Straight away I delivered a double palm strike, and before I knew it I was heading towards the wall. I bounced off the wall and quickly turned around to see his face in mine. He smiled and slapped me across the face, and then he walked away shaking his head. By this time I was very upset I could not believe what had just happened to me.

Once I had contained myself, then who should walk through the door, but Tonys' uncle. He walked straight over to Master Deng and started talking to him. I said to Tony "What is your uncle doing here?". He then replied "He wants to train with him as well". It was then when Tony told me that he is not just any old master, he is well respected in Shanghai and his father Deng Ke Yu was taught directly by Yang Cheng Fu of the Yang Style Tai Chi Chuan. He was also a very close friend of the renowned Cheng Man Ching, who later devised his own style.

Tony also told me that when Master Deng was younger he had studied many different internal martial arts such as Chen Style, Hsing Ye Chuan and Dat Mo Stick to name but a few. The reason that I am writing this book is to share with you the knowledge that was passed on to me from Master Deng. I have met many people who teach Tai Chi, especially within the Yang Style circles and their interpretation of the art has been quite amusing. I will not be delving into any other form of exercise or training methods to enhance my Tai Chi. I can assure you that Yang Style Tai Chi does not need any source of input or any other disciplines to make it more interesting. I will be talking about Yang Style Tai Chi, the martial art, and training in the shadow of a true master, DENG ER QIAN of Shanghai.

Master Deng Er Qian.

INSTRUCTOR - COACH

Over the past few years I have been asked by many people 'How do you find the right instructor or coach to learn Tai Chi from?'. This is very difficult to answer as you have to decide what you want from Tai Chi. Is it for traditional training such as the 'martial art', or just for health such as the 'breathing exercise', only you can decide this.

For me personally what I look for in a teacher is honesty and openness and 'that' little bit of magic. They need to know their Tai Chi form to the extent that they know how to apply each technique in a martial art context, not borrowing some other martial art technique such as 'application', to enhance their system. A teacher that does not mind being questioned, who has the openness to explain to you what each movement is for and how to apply it. If they can do this without any hesitation, then to me they have the magic. Master Deng has this magic.

Whenever we did pushing hands, we would always start off with 'Grasp the Birds Tail'. As we were going through this exercise I would ask him how to apply 'Part the Wild Horses Mane' in pushing hands. He would then straight away without any hesitation show how to apply this technique and he would say 'okay'. That is the magic of Deng Er Qian.

I remember once I was asked by a Tai Chi instructor to do some pushing hands with his student. We faced off with each other and both went into a 'ward off' position. His student dropped into a 'bow stance' posture. I looked at the instructor and said "What is going on?", he said "Try and push my student", I replied "But he is in a bow stance!". This meant his back leg was locked out, there was no central equilibrium, and so really all I could apply was either a 'roll back', a 'pull down', or an 'uproot' technique, but the teacher wanted me to push him directly straight ahead. I said this could not be done, so the instructor asked me to step aside, so I did and up he came. He placed both his hands onto his student's hands and suddenly his student went running backwards about 15 feet and hit a crash mat that was propped against a wall. I said to the teacher "I would appreciate it very much if you would do to me what you just did to your student?". I held up my hands but the teacher just walked away, so I asked "Where are you going?", he said "I cannot push you because you cannot feel the Chi". My answer to that teacher was "In Shanghai they can feel my Chi and in Hong Kong they can feel my Chi, so I am very sorry you have a problem with feeling it".

I know a lot of people out there would of thought this guy has incredible powers and strength. I have seen teachers just walk up to their students and just touch them and they fall to the floor screaming. Why are their students so gullible and what possesses them to react like this?. It is as if their teacher is brain washing them.

I have asked some of these teachers what would happen to them if they were in a real situation, their tricks would not save them. I often wonder how a lot of these people would measure up to some of my good friends around the world. You see, I live in the real world, you are in the wrong game if you do not like getting hurt, as Yang Style Tai Chi can be a very formidable martial art, but it is just like any other martial art you study, you have to work at it to get results. I have had students leave because of this, but nothing comes easy. I was once quoted by a good friend, he said:

'If you want to be a champion, then you have to train like one'.

I do not claim to know everything about Tai Chi you never stop learning. We have all been gullible and naive at some point in our lives, but when you put your trust into your teacher, you hope that he is steering you in the right direction. There are a lot of good teachers out there, but you will have to search for them and have a good look around before you make a final decision. Do not be scared to ask questions.

The reason that I have written this book is to be honest and straight to the point. This book is for the true martial artists and Tai Chi practitioners who want to explore beyond the 85 forms, single Pushing Hands or even Grasp the Bird's Tail. I want you to realise that there is a lot more to one particular style if you are prepared to dig deeper within the boundaries of that style.

If you ever have the opportunity to travel to Mainland China, i.e. Shanghai or Beijing, then you will see for yourself that what I talk about in this book is just a 'drop in the ocean'.

It is important to remember that when you find the right teacher they must also learn to trust you as a good-natured and sensible person, someone that they can trust to pass their knowledge on to.

Master Deng once told me that a book is   there as a reference only, not as a teacher.

SO GOOD LUCK and remember to

'train hard and win easy'.
Bob Fermor.

Bob Fermor with Master Deng Er Qian.

YANG STYLE TAI CHI CHUAN

Yang Style Tai Chi can be very complex and sometimes confusing, especially when learning Tai Chi for the very first time. It is at this point where your teacher plays a very important part in your early stages of training. It is also important to note that where most hard style Kung Fu systems takes an average of three years to learn, an internal system like Tai Chi can take up to ten years to become proficient.

Learning Yang Style Tai Chi from Master Deng was simplicity in itself. He always said 'Keep it simple and just breathe naturally to begin with and try to practise as much as you can. Always remember if you practise the same move over and over again or even a thousand times it would still not be enough'.

So let us look at Yang Style Tai Chi as taught to me by Master Deng:

1. The Yang 85 Forms.

2. The Yang broad Sword.

3. The Yang Straight Sword.

4. Pushing Hands.

Master Deng applying Cloud Hands in Tui Sau.

Pushing Hands training is without a doubt the most important of these four, simply because without it your Tai Chi form will only be a form of exercise, not the training of the true martial art. Pushing Hands is the link between the Long Form and the executing of a martial art technique in a 'real life or death' situation. The Long Form is where you practise the moves of the martial art techniques, co-ordination of breathe and learning to obtain a correct posture and Pushing Hands is where you learn to apply the techniques in an exercise, working together with a partner. Through this training method you will learn to feel and adhere to your partner, learning to sense when your partner is going to initiate an attack by feeling through your hands. This is also known as 'sticking and listening energy'.

REQUIREMENTS OF THE 85 FORMS

When learning the Yang long 85 forms, take your time and do not rush it. The 85 forms means exactly what it says, it is comprised of 85 moves, which means each part has a beginning and an ending. Every move in the form has a name i.e. 'Grasp the Bird's Tail', 'Single Whip', 'Part the Wild Horses Mane', and so on. The first form is called 'The Opening Form'. This is a good form to practise some of the basic Tai Chi requirements.

FORM 1 - OPENING FORM

a.   b.   c.

Note: Master Deng once told me that in Tai Chi there is a rhythm, e.g. when raising the arms slowly count to four, then repeat the count as you return the hands to where they began.

1: BASICS: In the opening form our feet should be shoulder width apart and our arms are held loosely by our sides. We slowly raise our arms to shoulder level, and then bend our elbows and knees together at the same time, returning our hands to where they began. At the same time our body is sinking into its first posture. This posture will be the level in which we intend to practise our form from beginning to end.

2: ROOT: We learn to tuck our bottom in so as to acquire a good root to the ground. By tucking, we pull in the coccyx, which pulls our spine into line, which then allows our Chi energy to travel up and down our spinal cord. Tucking not only provides a root and a strong posture, but also closes our anal passage to keep the vital energy enclosed within the 'Dan Tien' (which is situated roughly two inches below the naval). **See photo.**

3: VISION: Our eyes must always look afar, never up or down, always straight ahead, to enable us to use our peripheral vision.

4: EMPTINESS: We must learn to empty our mind and to think only of what we are doing within our form, and to disperse of any noises or interruptions that may occur around us.

5: BREATHING: As we raise and lower our arms and sink into our posture, we learn to co-ordinate our 'in-breath' and our 'out-breath'. This is achieved by breathing in as we raise our arms and breathing out as we lower our arms and sink into our posture. Please note that this is easy to apply in form one 'The Opening Form', but incorporating this into the other forms is more complex. Master Deng said to me 'when playing Tai Chi, just breathe naturally at first. If you try to co-ordinate your breathing with the form as a beginner, you could do more harm to your body than good as there is so much to take in at first (with the moving of the hands, the feet and the direction that you are moving in), that it is only when you can move naturally from one move to another that you can start to co-ordinate your breathing with your form.

6: OUTER THREE: When we talk about the bending of our elbows and knees at the same time, this brings us on to the 'outer three'. In theory this means simply that the wrist is connected to the ankle, the elbow is connected to the knee and the shoulder is connected to the hip. This means the body must move as one. This sounds easy but we must not forget that in the opening form there is no foot movement, so when you start to move, the application of the outer three is somewhat more difficult. In time and practise this can be achieved.

7: SPIRIT: The sign of a true master is in his eyes. Master Deng says 'this is your spirit. By looking into your opponent's eyes, you can tell whether his spirit is high or low', or in other words, is he strong, weak or is he confident within himself. The simplest way to notice any of these signs is if your opponent cannot look you straight in the eye. By him looking down he shows that he is weak and lacks confidence and is a person that does not believe in himself or his ability. Each movement performed in the Yang Long Form has a martial art application thus giving the form a meaning and a purpose as opposed to just breathing in and breathing out, for example: To apply the opening form, imagine you are being strangled. You raise your arms directly under the attackers, breaking their hold. By doing this, you automatically break his root; you then apply your counter attack with a double palm to the chest. You can imagine this at all times from the beginning of the form to the end. Each form that has a different name has a different martial art application. From an outsider looking in, all you are doing is going through a sequence of movements in a non-aggressive manner, like a dance. That is why Tai Chi (being an internal system) is like an iron bar covered in cotton wool. You only ever appreciate it as a martial art when you get hit by it.

8: CHI GONG: I once asked Master Deng to explain to me what is Chi Gong he laughed and replied "Tai Chi is Chi Gong and Chi Gong is Tai Chi they are both the same" We interpret the word 'Chi' as 'vital energy'. Blood is a vital energy as without it you die. Air is also a vital energy, without it you die. By combining the two and taking a deeper breath below the diaphragm you are allowing more oxygen into the blood stream. The oxygen in the blood stream then circulates around the body and nourishes the internal organs. It is important when you are practising a Chi Gong exercise (also known as 'cultivation of breath'), that your body should be rounded, allowing the blood to circulate. At no point should there be any sharp corners. This can be compared to a hosepipe with a kink in it, the water cannot flow. To practise Chi Gong within the opening form, simply just repeat the movement as many times as you like.

9: INNER THREE: In form one you can practise and apply the inner three. This is achieved by using the mind to generate your inner force at the base of the 'Dan Tien'. You then project your 'Chi' or 'Force' through the body channels and then out through the hands. This is noticeable when the force is being projected through the hands, the fingers   start to shake through natural tension. This is also known as 'Firing', 'Far Ging' or 'Lick'.

10: CHI: The time will come when you will ask yourself "when will I feel my Chi?", all I can say is you will know. I guarantee that once you can incorporate all of the requirements that I have spoken about in the opening form, you can then start to relax the body, which   will relieve tension within the muscles. You will feel a warm and tingly sensation running through the body. To emphasise this in more depth: The nervous system becomes so acute to the body structure that you can actually feel the blood circulating around the body. The hands will get warm and if you let the palms of your hands face each other, you will feel a magnetic pull between them. When you release the Chi, (this is normally executed at the end of each form), you will feel that the hands tend to shake because of the natural tension that has formulated within the movement. By releasing it, will enable you to relax the body and carry on to the next form.

11: UP ROOTING: Now you can apply your first training exercise. Get your partner to stand opposite you and stand with your feet shoulder width apart. Let them grab both of your wrists, (make sure their arms are straight). Now keeping your arms straight, just raise them up. Remember to tuck and then watch just how easy it is to uproot your partner. **see photos.**

a   b

Once we move onto the rest of the forms from 'the Opening Form', the 11 requirements that we have just spoken about must also be applied to these forms. Once the form is in motion, there are still further requirements that should also be applied.

12: HOLD THE BALL: This is a transitional movement in between each form to help the forms move from one to another. In Tai Chi we call this 'continuity', there should be no stops. The ball represents the 'in-breath', and in martial arts the Chinese use the theory of 'the world spinning on its axis'. This is like a steel rod running through the centre of a ball allowing it to turn, an attacker strikes the ball causing the ball to spin, which deflects the attacker into emptiness. When this is applied in a martial art context the defender will turn at the hips just like the ball. They will then simultaneously strike the attacker with their energy or

holding the ball

force resulting in double impact. Double impact means a defender deflects whilst utilising their attackers energy or force to defeat ones self. The attacker strikes the defender who deflects their force, leaving the attacker vulnerable and unbalanced. It is at this point that the defender will apply their counter attack.

13: LEGWORK: Your legs define the level that you want to practise your Tai Chi form on. A lower posture will allow you to strengthen your legs, giving you a strong root. You will soon learn how to distribute your weight from one leg to the other. In Kung-Fu they use a posture called 'Ma-Po', (Horse-Riding Stance). Their theory behind this posture is 'to train in Ma-Po will give you a strong foundation'. It is like a house built on concrete, it is strong, if you build it on sand it will fall down. So whether it is Tai Chi or Kung-Fu, 'Ma-Po' plays a very important part.

14: FOOT WORK: When going through your Tai Chi form, you will encounter various footwork patterns. First of all you will notice the turning of the foot, which is normally 45°. This is normally applied on the transitional movement from one form to another. The reasons being: (a) With your body also being at a 45° angle, this automatically protects your centre line where your main primary targets are located. (b) Turning the foot 45° will also keep your Knee in line with your toes, this avoids unnecessary pressure or strain on the knee joint. The footwork that is incorporated within the Tai Chi form helps to practise the form at a slower pace. Mostly the footwork is heel then toe, but there are also other variations, for example, side stepping (performed in Cloud Hands), where the toe is placed down first, stepping backwards (performed in Repulse the Monkey), where the toe is placed down first.

There are also half-steps performed in White Crane Spreads its Wings, Strum the Lute, Fist Under Elbow and Raise Hands. A half step is when you bring your right foot behind your left. I was informed by Master Deng that a half step was originally performed as a vigorous stamping motion to add more power and speed when executing a technique. These however, were taken out as the repetitive use of stamping (whilst practicing the form) was too demanding on the body, although I might add, the stamping has remained within the weapon forms (Yang Broad Sword and Yang Straight Sword).

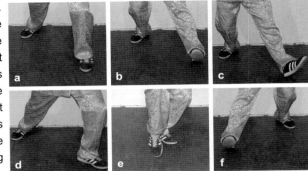

footwork pattern

15: HIPS & WAIST: The hips and waist play a very important part within the Tai Chi form. It is said that 'the hip proceeds the movement', which means by utilising this movement and maintaining a strong root, you can produce maximum power through the looseness of the waist. This enables the upper body to move more freely and helps to generate 'Far Ging'.

16: ELASTICITY: With the hips preceding the movement, this action also forms elasticity. This helps the form to flow in a continuous motion from one form to another with no sudden stops. Elasticity can also be interpreted as opening and closing or contracting and expanding. Contracting and expanding is a movement you will incorporate by using a recoil motion which will generate a force of explosive power also known as 'Far Ging' or 'Firing'. This particular action can be seen applied in many other Chinese martial art systems.

17: POSTURE: Holding a correct posture is very important when practising your Tai Chi form. First keep your elbows pointing downwards. This is very important as this will provide quick protection to the floating ribs area. There is an old Chinese saying, 'by striking to your opponents ribs, you are stealing his breath'. We know this as winding your opponent, so by keeping the elbows pointing downwards, we can retract the arms at any given time. I have seen many Tai Chi practitioners playing Tai Chi with their elbows held high to allow their 'Chi' to flow more easily around the body. For health this is okay, but for martial arts this is not acceptable. By keeping the elbows pointing downwards and creating a space under the armpit, this still allows the 'Chi' to flow. **See photos.**

18: P`ENG: P'eng translates as 'ward off', it is a guarding posture and also the space that is created between your hand and your body. Testing your P'eng is a very important part of your Tai Chi training. This can be achieved very easily, for example: If you are holding the P'eng posture from 'Grasp the Bird's Tail', get a partner to push against your arm. Do not make the mistake of getting your partner to push against your body, as you must remember that it is your centre line (where the primary targets are), which you are protecting from your attacker. Points to remember:

1. Your weight should be distributed equally formulating 'central equilibrium.

2. Tuck in your bottom, bringing your coccyx inline with your spinal cord. This will automatically give you a strong root to the ground.

3. At the same time you will be holding out your arm with the back of your hand facing your partner and palm facing your centre line. Create the space between your hand and your body.

4. By concentrating on your tucking at the base of the spine, the space created between your hand and your body (P`eng), becomes very strong.

Note: Never hold a bow stance posture when testing your P'eng, this is not acceptable. See photos below.

19: TESTING: Testing of the other postures can also be applied, but you must remember that each posture is a martial art application. To test each posture, you must test it at the end of the movement, which will also be your out-breath.

You must test the hand that is applying the technique. It is important to remember that P`eng is formulated in every movement, so when testing the structure it should be rounded and strong and well rooted. Your strongest point will always be where the technique is being executed, that will be the place to test your posture. Master Deng made a point of saying that, 'if you test your posture by pushing against the body (the centre line), then why bother with P`eng'.

P`eng is like a guard, it is your boundary of protection and no one should penetrate it. That is why pushing hands is implemented in your training. This exercise is to train for just that, you must protect your centre line at all times. By feeling through your opponent's hands, you can then feel an attack being executed. Most Chinese martial arts have this exercise, not just Tai Chi, but you might know it as 'Sticking Hands'. It is all the same, you are learning to adhere to your opponent and to penetrate ones defence.

Please note that the testing of this posture (Single Whip), is on the left open palm and not the right hand which is formulating the cranes beak.

20: NINE POINTS: There are nine points on our body that help to formulate maximum power from the postures root. By utilising the nine points, you can project your force through the body. It is these nine points that give you your maximum power, the end result being - 'Far Ging'.

1: ANKLE	**4: LOWER SPINE**	**7: SHOULDER**
2: KNEE	**5: MIDDLE SPINE**	**8: ELBOW**
3: HIP	**6: UPPER SPINE**	**9: WRIST**

As you can see from the photo below, Jordan is applying 'Brush Knee Push'. To apply the nine points, you would start from the transitional movement, which would be 'hold the ball' posture, your weight is on your right leg. It is at this point (as you step forward with your left leg), that you start to apply the nine points in order as you execute Brush Knee Push.

Jordan Fermor - 6 years old

31

21: FIVE BOW : The five bow is a technique that is also used to generate maximum force or 'Far Ging' through the body. This is achieved through the spine, and both the elbows and the knees. For example: As you expand the body on the out-breath, both arms would be driving forwards, as the spine pushes backwards. This is like driving a wedge into the middle of a stone, as the two parts separate they shoot off into two opposite directions. The wedge that is driven downwards would represent the force that we use to generate through our knees and elbows.

22: TIGER'S MOUTH : The tiger's mouth is formulated by the shape of the hand, as you can see in the **photo below, right.** The four fingers are held together and the thumb is kept apart to formulate the tiger's mouth. By utilising the tiger's mouth, we can apply locking and grabbing techniques at any given time.

Being struck by the open hand palm will do more internal damage than a fist, which will do more external damage. You will find that after a period of time when practising Yang Tai Chi, the tiger's mouth will formulate and become more natural. The index finger starts to break away from the other three fingers. It is very common to see this in practitioners that have played Tai Chi for many years. Master Deng once told me that you can guide the direction of your Chi through your index finger.

FAR GING - EXERCISES

Far Ging is the end product of ones force in an attack. This force is formulated internally by utilising the body in a spiralling motion, which is also known as 'the entwinings', which can be accomplished by utilising two opposite forces. These forces are normally generated with an upward and a downward motion. The main source of this energy or force is produced from the waist. On impact the force is explosive and this can only ever be achieved through timeless practice. It is as I have mentioned before, by utilising the five bow technique in conjunction with the nine points, Far Ging can be achieved.

Above: Bob Fermor is demonstrating the nunchakus at the Super Seminar. As you can see he demonstrates explosive power to the maximum. Whether it is with a weapon or open hand, this can still be known as Far Ging. In this photograph it was estimated that the nunchakus are travelling at approximately _120 mph_.

FAR GING - FIRING EXERCISES - KICKING

When practising these exercises, you have to implement the outer three first. As you can see in the photographs the whole body moves as one. Start off slowly and then speed it up without any tension in the body. When you are balancing on your leg to execute your kick, the arms separate precisely at the same time as the leg extends. You will know when you get this right as the body starts to shake. This is the force that is being executed through the kick. **You can repeat this exercise as many times as you like.**

FAR GING - FIRING EXERCISES
PRESSING (five bow)

This exercise is good to implement the five bow. On the in-breath the hands circle downwards to the Dan Tien, then upwards towards the chest and on the out-breath you are ready to execute Far Ging. As the hands push forwards on the out-breath, the spine is pushing backwards. As this exercise speeds up, you will start to charge forwards and by raising the leading leg will enable you to maintain your tuck and keep a strong posture. **You can repeat this exercise as many times as you like.**

FAR GING - FIRING EXERCISES
OFF THE WALL (five bow)

This exercise is also good to implement the five bow theory. Face off against a wall and keep the arms and legs slightly bent at the elbows and knees. Without any hesitation, quickly straighten the arms and legs, but there must be no tension within the body at all. You will find that you can project your body backwards with great force. You will find that this exercise can be a bit disorientating at first and you will hesitate to implement the push, but with practice this will become more explosive and natural. If you like you can have a partner to catch you as you come off the wall. **You can repeat this exercise as many times as you like.**

FAR GING - UPROOTING EXERCISE
(Brush Knee Push)

If your partner is in a left fighting stance and attacks with a reverse punch to your centre line, by utilising 'Brush Knee Push', you re-direct the attack to the left. By doing this you open up their centre line. As you counter attack with a right palm heel strike, the fingers will make contact first, this is like feeling. Once this contact has been made, you will now start to adhere to our opponent by initiating a palm heel strike. This force is driven through your opponent making his posture weak at the root. By following through in an upward motion, adhering to your opponent at all times, you will uproot your opponent driving him backwards. So remember, feel, break and uproot. **Master Deng once said 'that to defeat your opponent you must first become one'.**

Ben Fermor - 15 years old

Joanne Fermor - Yang straight sword
Bird flying to roost

Traditional
WARM UP (exercises)
of the
Nine points

Grand Master Deng Ke Yu in Shanghai

This section demonstrates a traditional warm up routine, which is normally practised prior to your Tai Chi forms. It can also be used as a warm down routine.

Warm up -1
Basic warm up

This exercise is a basic warm up. As you can see, the photos are showing you which parts of the body to strike.

To get this exercise in motion, you must co-ordinate the bending of the knees with the striking point of the body. If you look at photos 1 & 2, you can see a rise and fall in the body movement, for example: In the first photo the legs are straight and in the second photo the knees are bent. Whatever part of the body you are striking, the knees should be bent. To get this exercise in motion, start off by striking the thighs 3 times before moving on to striking the knees.

The benefits of this exercise are to invigorate and improve the blood circulation and to warm up the body and the muscles. **Repeat this exercise as many times as you like.**

1. Ready position

2. Striking thighs front

3. Striking knees

4. Striking shins

Master Deng pointed out that actions always speak louder than words. It is a well-known fact that a picture paints a thousand words, we therefore cannot emphasise enough how important it is to study the photos carefully, both in this section and throughout the book.

5. Striking calves

6. Striking thighs back

7. Striking bottom

8. Striking lower spine

9. Striking abdomen

10. Resume position

Warm up - 2
Swinging arms

In this exercise you are striking to the shoulder and to the lower part of the spine together at the same time. Also as you strike these two points, you transfer your body weight from one leg to the other and turn at the waist.

Note: When the arms are swinging they are held at shoulder level.

In photo 1, the body is in motion. The arms are swinging and the body weight is transferring to the right leg

In photo 2, the right palm is striking the left shoulder and the back of the left hand is striking the lower part of the spine.

The benefits of all these exercises, are to relieve any built up stress and strain on the meridian points of your body. By striking these points, you are helping the Chi to flow more easily around the nervous system and the meridian channels.

Also by striking these points, you will enable the blood to circulate around your body more freely, helping to nourish your internal organs.

In photo 3, the body is now in motion, the arms are swinging and the body weight is transferring to the left leg.

In photo 4, the left palm is striking the right shoulder and the back of the right hand is striking the lower part of the spine.

Continue with the exercise and repeat as many times as you like.

Warm up - 3
Strike top of spine & under arm pit

In photo 1, feet are shoulder width apart and hands held loosely at your sides. you raise your arms, palms facing upwards.

In photo 2, strike your left palm over your left shoulder to the top of the spine and at the same time strike under the armpit with your right palm.

Brandon Fermor - 15 months old

In photo 3, your swing your arms downwards, bending your knees at the same time, then swing your arms upwards, palms facing up.

3

In photo 4, as the legs straighten, strike your right palm over your right shoulder to the top of the spine, and at the same time strike under the armpit with your left palm.

4

Warm up - 4
Strike top of spine & centre of spine
& massage the kidneys

Joanne demonstrating the spear at Pontins holiday camp, Blackpool.

In photo 1, feet are shoulder width apart and hands held loosely at your sides, raise your arms palms facing upwards.

In photo 2, as the legs straighten, both palms circle upwards over the right & left shoulder to strike to the top of the spine.

In photo 3, now circle both palms downwards bending both knees at the same time.

In photo 4, turn both palms into fists and as you straighten your legs, strike the centre of the spine.

Back profile

In photo 5, open both palms and apply pressure to the kidney area.

Back profile

5

In photo 6, as you start to straighten the legs, both palms rotate to face upwards. End of exercise. **Repeat as many times as you like.**

Back profile

6

Warm up - 5
Striking the knee & lower spine

In photo 1, turn your body to the left, right palm facing downwards and the back of the left hand is aiming to strike to the lower spine.

In photo 2, bending the right leg, apply pressure to the inside of the left knee with your right knee. The right palm is striking to the outside of the knee precisely at the same time. The left hand is also striking to the lower spine at the same time. Co-ordinate the three moves together.

In photo 3, turn your body to the right, the left palm facing downwards and the back of the right hand is aiming to strike to the lower spine.

In photo 4, bending the left leg, apply pressure to the inside of the right knee with your left knee. The left palm is striking to the outside of the knee precisely at the same time. The right hand is also striking to the lower spine at the same time. Coordinate the three moves together.

Warm up - 6
Striking the ankles

In photo 1, feet are shoulder width apart, turn your body to the left with your right arm stretched above your head, palm facing downwards. The back of the left hand is aiming to strike to the lower spine.

In photo 2, the right palm strikes down to the left ankle at the same time as the left hand strikes to the lower spine.

It is important to co-ordinate these two moves precisely at the same time.

In photo 3, turn your body to the right with your left arm stretched above your head, palm facing downwards. The back of the right hand is aiming to strike to the lower spine.

In photo 4, the left palm strikes down to the right ankle at the same time as the right hand strikes to the lower spine.

It is important to co-ordinate these two moves precisely at the same time.

Warm up - 7
Striking the elbow & wrist

In photo 1, the right palm strikes upwards to the left wrist in a circular motion.

In photo 2, the right hand then circles around in a clockwise motion.

In photo 3, the right palm strikes the left elbow.

You can repeat this exercise as many times as you like on the one side.

In photo 4, left palm is striking upwards to the right wrist in a circular motion.

In photo 5, the left hand then circles around in an anti-clockwise motion.

In photo 6, the left palm strikes the right elbow.

You can repeat this exercise as many times as you like on the one side.

Stretching - 1

1. Step forward with the left leg and then stretch upwards with both palms.
2. Pull up the right knee and grasp with both palms tuck in at the coccyx and hold your posture for as long as you like. **Repeat this exercise on the opposite side, see photos 3 & 4.**

Stretch 1

Stretching - 2 & 3

It is important to have good flexibility when practising Yang Style Tai Chi. Stretch 1&2 help to improve this, the main part of the body being stretched here is the hamstring.

Stretch 2

Stretch 3

 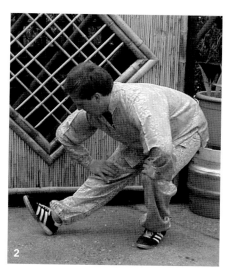

Traditional Yang 85 Forms

Section 1

1. Opening Form
2. Step Up (Shoulder Stroke) Grasp the Bird's Tail
3. Single Whip
4. Raise Hands
5. White Crane Spreads its Wings
6. Brush Knee, Push
7. Strum the Lute
8. Brush Knee, Push 3 times

9. Strum the Lute
10. Brush Knee, Push
11. Step Up Parry Punch
12. Apparent Close Up
13. Cross Hands

Section 2

14. Carry the Tiger to the Mountain
15. Fist Under Elbow
16. Repulse the Monkey 3, 5 or 7 times
17. Slant Flying
18. Raise Hands

19. White Crane Spreads its Wings
20. Brush Knee, Push

21. Needle at Sea Bottom
22. Flash Arm
23. Turn, Sidle Punch
24. Step Up Parry Punch

25. Step Up Grasp the Bird's Tail
26. Single Whip
27. Cloud Hands 3, 5 or 7 times
28. Single Whip
29. High Pat on Horse
30. Separate Right Foot
31. Separate Left Foot
32. Turn Kick Left Heel
33. Brush Knee, Push 2 times
34. Brush Knee, Downward Punch
35. Turn, Sidle Punch
36. Step Up Parry Punch
37. Kick Right Heel
38. Hit the tiger to the Left and Right
39. Kick Right Heel
40. Strike Opponent with Fists

41. Kick Left Heel, Turn 360°
42. Kick Right Heel
43. Step Up Parry Punch
44. Apparent Close Up
45. Cross Hands

Pictures Grandmaster Deng Ke Yu

Section 3

46. Carry the Tiger to the Mountain
47. Diagonal Single Whip
48. Part the Wild Horses Mane 3 times
49. Step Up (Shoulder Stroke) Grasp the Bird's Tail

50. Single Whip
51. Fair Lady Works the Shuttles to the 4 corners
52. Step Up (Shoulder Stroke) Grasp the Bird's Tail
53. Single Whip
54. Cloud Hands 3, 5 or 7 times
55. Single Whip
56. Snake Creeps Down
57. Golden Rooster Stands on Left & Right Legs
58. Repulse the Monkey 3, 5 or 7 times

59. Slant Flying
60. Raise Hands
61. White Crane Spreads its Wings
62. Brush Knee, Push
63. Needle at Sea Bottom

64. Flash Arm

65. Turn, Sidle Punch, Snake Shows its Tongue
66. Step Up Parry Punch
67. Step Up Grasp the Bird's Tail
68. Single Whip
69. Cloud Hands 3, 5 or 7 times
70. Single Whip
71. High Pat on Horse
72. Floating Palm
73. Turn, Kick Right Heel
74. Step Up Parry Downward Punch
75. Step Up Grasp the Bird's Tail
76. Single Whip
77. Snake Creeps Down
78. Form the Seven Stars
79. Retreat to Ride the Tiger
80. Turn, White Lotus Kick
81. Archer Shooting the Tiger

82. Step Up Parry Punch
83. Apparent Close Up
84. Cross Hands
85. Closing Form

White Crane Spreading
its Wings

Traditional Yang 85 Forms
SECTION 1
(Forms 1 through to 13)

Master Deng in Shanghai

FORM 1 - OPENING FORM

1a. Your hands are held loosely by your sides, your feet are shoulder width apart and you look afar (straight ahead).

1b. Raise your hands shoulder level.

1c. Bend your elbows and knees at the same time.

1d. Your hands return to your sides as your body sinks down. This will be the level that your Tai Chi form will be performed at.

1a   relax the mind

1b

1c

1d

FORM 2 - STEP UP (Shoulder Stroke)
GRASP THE BIRD'S TAIL

2a. Your body weight transfers to your left leg, your right foot turns out 45°. Transfer your weight to your right leg and pull in your left foot. Your left hand moves to hip level, palm facing up, at the same time the right hand circles on the inside to shoulder level, palm facing down. This is known as **'hold the ball'**.

2b. Your left foot steps out, (North). Rotate your hips to formulate shoulder stroke.

2c. Turn your hips, bring in your right foot while forming **(hold the ball)**.

2d. Step away with your right foot and ward off, **(P'eng)**.

2a

2b   (Shoulder Stroke)

2c

2d   (Ward Off - P'eng)

2e. Turn your right palm down and your left palm up. Roll back **(Lu)** by dropping your left hand to your hip, whilst bringing your right hand into your shoulder, turning the palm inwards, as you transfer your weight to your left leg.

2f. & 2g. As your body weight is on your left leg, raise your left hand and place your palm onto your right wrist and then by pushing from your left leg, your weight is transferred to your right leg. This is called pressing, **(Ghi).**

2h. Your left hand slides over the top of your right hand both palms facing downwards.

2e   (Roll Back- Lu)   2f   (Pressing - Ghi)

2g   2h

2i

2i. Transfer your weight to your left leg and let the elbows drop slightly, (both palms are still facing downwards).

2j. By pushing from your left leg, transfer your body weight to your right leg, at the same time extend your arms slightly forwards, both palms facing forwards. This is called pushing, **(An)**.

2j   **(Pushing - An)**

FORM 3 - SINGLE WHIP

3a. Transfer your weight to your left leg to allow your right foot to turn inwards 45° on your heel. With palms facing downwards and arms held at shoulder level, rotate in an anti-clockwise circular motion.

3b. Drop your palms down to your hips (whilst carrying on with the circular motion), transfer your weight to your right leg. Raise your right hand to shoulder level and form a cranes beak, your left hand remains at your waist, palm facing upwards. At the same time pull in your left leg onto your toe.

3a

3b

3c

3c. Step away with your left leg in the direction of West, your left hand turns outwards, palm facing West.

FORM 4 - RAISE HANDS

4a. Your weight stays on your left leg as you bring in your right leg. You look in the direction of North as you turn your hips and place your right foot onto your heel in the direction of North, at the same time your right and left hands move into your centre line. Your left hand is now inline with your right elbow.

4a

FORM 5 - WHITE CRANE SPREADS ITS WINGS

5a. Pull back your right leg placing your foot onto your toe. Your right arm is formulating P'eng. Your left hand circles around to shoulder level.

5b. Your right leg steps forwards to the direction of North, allowing your body weight to transfer from your left to your right leg, at the same time your right arm drops, allowing you to apply shoulder stroke.

5a

5b

5c

5c. Now turn your body to the direction of West. Place your left foot onto your toe in front of your right foot. Your left palm is facing downwards and your right palm is facing upwards, **(hold the ball).**

5d. Your left hand drops down to hip level as you raise your right hand above your head to formulate White Crane.

5d

alternative angle

FORM 6 - BRUSH KNEE, PUSH

6a. Your right hand drops down to your hip, palm facing upwards. Your left hand circles up to your right shoulder, palm facing down, **(hold the ball).**

6b. Your right hand rises up to shoulder level as your left leg lifts up ready to step forwards onto your heel.

6a

6b

6c

6c. Place your left foot down heel first and as you transfer your weight to your left leg, your left hand sweeps across your left knee, palm facing downwards and your right palm pushes forwards.

FORM 7 - STRUM THE LUTE

7a. Your right leg steps up behind your left leg and you transfer your body weight to your right leg. Your left hand starts to raise and your right hand starts to pull in towards your centre line.

7b. Your left leg moves forwards placing your left foot onto your heel. As your right hand pulls inwards, place it beside your left elbow. Your left hand is in front of your right hand, both hands held at shoulder level.

FORM 8 - BRUSH KNEE, PUSH
(3 times)

8a. Pull back your left leg onto your toe and drop your right hand to hip level, your left hand sweeps across to your right shoulder, **(hold the ball)**. Your right hand rises up to shoulder level as your left leg lifts up ready to step forwards onto your heel.

8b. Place your left foot down heel first and as you transfer your weight to your left leg, your left hand sweeps across your left knee, palm facing downwards and your right palm pushes forwards.

8c. Sit back by putting your weight onto your right leg. This allows you to turn your left foot out 45°. Your right hand sweeps across to your left shoulder, palm facing downwards, your left palm just turns upwards at hip level, **(hold the ball).**

8d. Your right foot circles in towards your left foot as your left hand lifts up to your left shoulder (palm still facing upwards). Your right palm is still facing downwards.

8e. Place your right foot down heel first and as you transfer your weight to your right leg, your right hand sweeps across your right knee, palm facing downwards and your left palm pushes forwards.

8f. Sit back by putting your weight onto your left leg. This allows you to turn your right foot out 45°. Your left hand sweeps across to your right shoulder, palm facing downwards, your right palm just turns upwards at hip level, **(hold the ball).**

8g. Your left foot circles in towards your right foot as your right hand lifts up to your right shoulder (palm still facing upwards). Your left palm is still facing downwards.

8h. Place your left foot down heel first and as you transfer your weight to your left leg, your left hand sweeps across your left knee, palm facing downwards and your right palm pushes forwards.

FORM 9 - STRUM THE LUTE

9a. Your right leg steps up behind your left leg and you transfer your body weight to your right leg. Your left hand starts to raise and your right hand starts to pull in towards your centre line.

9b. Your left leg moves forwards placing your left foot onto your heel. As your right hand pulls inwards, place it beside your left elbow. Your left hand is in front of your right hand, both hands held at shoulder level.

FORM 10 - BRUSH KNEE, PUSH

10a. Pull back your left leg onto your toe and drop your right hand to hip level, your left hand sweeps across to your right shoulder, **(hold the ball)**. Your right hand rises up to shoulder level as your left leg lifts up ready to step forwards onto your heel.

10b. Place your left foot down heel first and as you transfer your weight to your left leg, your left hand sweeps across your left knee, palm facing downwards and your right palm pushes forwards.

FORM 11 - STEP UP PARRY PUNCH

11a. Sit back by putting your weight onto your right leg. This allows you to turn your left foot out 45°. Your right hand drops down to your hip palm facing upwards, your left hand lifts up to shoulder level palm facing downwards, **(hold the ball).**

11b. Step through with your right leg onto your heel, your right palm turns into a fist and is supported at your wrist by your left hand, circle the hands forwards.

11c. Transfer your weight to your right leg, lift your left leg and step through onto your heel. Your left hand slides forwards, palm facing forwards, as your right fist pulls back towards your hip.

11d. Transfer your weight to your left leg and at the same time punch forwards with your right fist, your left palm stays where it is.

FORM 12 - APPARENT CLOSE UP

12a. Your left hand slides under your right elbow. Your right fist opens, palm facing upwards.

12b. Your left hand slides up your right arm to the palm, both palms face upwards at shoulder level and open to shoulder width apart.

12c. Sit back transferring your weight to your right leg, drop your elbows slightly to turn your palms inwards to face each other.

12d. By pushing from your right leg, transfer your body weight to your left leg. At the same time push forwards with both palms.

12a

12b

12c

12d

FORM 13 - CROSS HANDS

13a

13a. By turning at your hips, you transfer your body weight to your right leg. This allows you to turn your left foot in 45° on your heel. Your right hand is circling towards your right shoulder, your left hand stays where it is. The body is now facing towards the direction of North.

13b. Transfer your body weight to your left leg and slide back your right foot so as they now become parallel. Both feet are shoulder width apart. At the same time both hands circle downwards and cross in front of the body, raising to shoulder level. Your left hand should be on the inside.

End of Section One

13b

Yang Style Applications

of

SECTION 1

Grandmaster Deng Ke Yu - in Shanghai

This technique is a counter attack from a strangle. As the strangle is applied raise both arms to break strangle and then push with double palms to the chest.

Opening Form

This is a counter attack from a punch. As the punch comes in you grab the wrist with your right hand and then come underneath with a shoulder stroke to the attackers floating ribs.

Shoulder Stroke

The right hand forms a cranes beak so it can hook on and deflect an incoming punch, whilst at the same time striking the attackers chest with the left palm.

Single Whip

The objective is to break the arm & leg and then uproot your opponent by locking the arm.

Raise Hands

This is a counter to a strangle. As the strangle is applied, break the strangle and kick to the groin at the same time.

White Crane Spreads its Wings

This is a counter to a mid section punch.
Block the punch outwards with your left hand and palm heel strike to the sternum with your right palm.

Brush Knee, Push

The objective is to break the leg, then swiftly pull your opponent down.

Strum the Lute

This is a counter to a punch. Parry the blow, kick to the knee then step through and punch to the floating ribs.

Step Up Parry Punch

The left hand comes underneath to sweep away the opponents right punch and to open up the centre line (main target area), for a double palm strike.

Apparent Close Up

This is a counter to a right punch. The right hand circles clockwise. Apply an outer block, then trap the attackers right arm to the inside of the right knee and throw the attacker over.

Cross Hands

Kick Right Heel

Traditional Yang 85 Forms
SECTION 2
(Forms 14 through to 45)

Master Deng in Shanghai

FORM 14 - CARRY THE TIGER TO THE MOUNTAIN

14a. Transfer your weight to your right leg and turn your left foot inwards on your heel 45°. Drop your left hand down to your hip, palm facing upwards, right palm faces downwards, **(hold the ball).**

14b. Lift up your right leg and at the same time raise your left arm shoulder level. Right palm still faces downwards.

14c. Step to the direction of South East. Your right palm sweeps across your right knee, palm facing downwards and your left palm pushes forwards.

14d. Your right palm circles inwards towards your Dan Tien, palm still facing downwards.

14e. Your right palm continues circling upwards towards shoulder level, then turn your palm to face forwards.

14f. Turn your right palm down and your left palm up. Roll back **(Lu)** by dropping your left hand to your hip, whilst bringing your right hand into your shoulder, turning the palm inwards, as you transfer your weight to your left leg.

14g. & 14h. As your body weight is on your left leg, raise your left hand and place your palm onto your right wrist and then by pushing from your left leg, your weight is transferred to your right leg. Pressing, **(Ghi).**

14d

14e

14f   (Roll Back - Lu)

14g   (Pressing - Ghi)

14i. Your left hand slides over the top of your right hand and the hands open to shoulder width apart, both palms facing downwards.

14j. Transfer your weight to your left leg and drop your elbows slightly, (both palms are still facing downwards).

14k. By pushing from your left leg, transfer your body weight to your leading leg and at the same time turn both palms forwards and push. Pushing, **(An).**

14h   (Pressing - Ghi)

14i

14j

14k   (Pushing - An)

FORM 15 - FIST UNDER ELBOW

15a. Transfer your weight to your left leg and turn your right foot in 45º. With both hands held at shoulder level palms facing downwards, rotate in an anti-clockwise circular motion.

15b. Both palms drop down towards your hips carrying on the circular motion.

15c. Transferring your weight to your right leg, step forward with your left leg in the direction of West, whilst still circling the hands.

15d. Now transfer your weight to your left leg and step up behind with your right foot. Your right hand raises to shoulder level, palm facing down and your left hand turns up at hip level, palm facing upwards, **(hold the ball).**

15a

15b

15c

15d

15e. You then transfer your weight to your right leg as you step up behind, your left leg then steps forwards, placing your left foot onto your heel. Your left hand circles up on the inside to shoulder level. You then push away with your left palm and as your right hand is travelling downwards on the outside, it then turns into a fist, which is placed under your left elbow.

15e

FORM 16 - REPULSE THE MONKEY
(3, 5 or 7 times)

16a. Your weight is fully on your right leg as you raise both palms upwards to shoulder level. Your left foot changes from heel to toe and you step backwards in the direction of East with your left leg.

16b. As you step back with your left leg, bend your right arm at the elbow and bring in your right hand towards your face.

16a

16b

16c

16c. By turning at your hips, transfer your weight to your left leg. Your left hand pulls back into your hip, palm facing upwards and your right hand pushes forwards, palm facing forwards. At the same time, turn in your right foot on the heel, so that your toe is facing forwards.

16d. All of your weight is on your left leg as you raise both palms upwards to shoulder level.

16e. As you step back with your right leg, bend your left arm at the elbow and bring in your left hand towards your face.

16f. By turning at your hips, transfer your weight to your right leg. Your right hand pulls back into your hip, palm facing upwards and your left hand pushes forwards, palm facing forwards. At the same time, turn in your left foot on the heel, so that your toe is facing forwards.

16g. All of your weight is on your right leg as you raise both palms upwards to shoulder level.

16h. As you step back with your left leg, bend your right arm at the elbow and bring in your right hand towards your face.

16i. By turning at your hips, transfer your weight to your left leg. Your left hand pulls back into your hip, palm facing upwards and your right hand pushes forwards, palm facing forwards. At the same time, turn in your right foot on the heel, so that your toe is facing forwards.

FORM 17 - SLANT FLYING

17a. Your left hand raises up to shoulder level, palm facing down. Your right hand circles downwards to your hip, palm facing up. At the same time, your right foot pulls in, in front of your left foot, resting on your toe, **(hold the ball).**

17b. Step out on your heel in the direction of North East, with your right leg.

17a

17b

17c

17c. Transfer your weight to your right leg and stretch forwards with your right arm to shoulder level, palm facing upwards. Your left hand drops to your hip, palm facing downwards.

FORM 18 - RAISE HANDS

18a. Your left foot steps up behind your right foot and as you transfer your weight to your left leg, your right foot steps forwards onto your heel. Your right and left hands move into your centre line. Your left hand is now inline with your right elbow.

18a

FORM 19 - WHITE CRANE SPREADS ITS WINGS

19a. Pull back your right leg placing your foot onto your toe. Your right arm is formulating P'eng. Your left hand circles around to shoulder level.

19b. Your right leg steps forwards to the direction of North, allowing your body weight to transfer from your left to your right leg, at the same time your right arm drops, allowing you to apply shoulder stroke.

19a

19b

19c

19c. Now turn your body to the direction of West. Place your left foot onto your toe in front of your right foot. Your left palm is facing downwards and your right palm is facing upwards, **(hold the ball).**

19d. Your left hand drops down to hip level as you raise your right hand above your head to formulate White Crane.

19d

alternative angle

FORM 20 - BRUSH KNEE, PUSH

20a. Your right hand drops down to your hip, palm facing upwards. Your left hand circles up to your right shoulder, palm facing down, **(hold the ball).**

20b. Your right hand rises up to shoulder level as your left leg lifts up ready to step forwards onto your heel.

20c. Place your left foot down heel first and as you transfer your weight to your left leg, your left hand sweeps across your left knee, palm facing downwards and your right palm pushes forwards.

FORM 21 - NEEDLE AT SEA BOTTOM

21a. Step up with your right foot behind your left foot, transferring your weight to your right leg. Your left hand raises to touch your right wrist, both hands raise to shoulder level.

21b. Both hands circle in towards your chest, lifting up your left foot at the same time. You then place your left foot down onto your toe as your left hand sweeps across your left knee. The fingers of your right hand point directly down towards the floor.

101

FORM 22 - FLASH ARM

22a. Your left hand again touches your right wrist, raise both hands to shoulder level. As your body weight is still on your right leg, step forwards with your left leg and place your left foot down onto your heel.

22b. As you transfer your weight to your left leg, your right palm turns upwards and your arm raises above your head, at the same time your left palm pushes forwards.

FORM 23 - TURN, SIDLE PUNCH

East

23a. Transfer your weight to your right leg and turn in your left foot 45°. Turning your hips to the direction of East, your right hand forms a fist and drops to hip level whilst your left hand raises up above your head, palm facing upwards.

23b. Pull in your right hand towards your body, raising it up towards your left shoulder. Your left hand circles down on the outside of your right arm to your left hip, at the same time you transfer your weight to your left leg and pull in your right foot onto your toe.

23c. Carrying on with the circular motion, your right fist pushes out to shoulder level as you step forwards with your right leg.

23d. Your left palm raises up the side of your body to shoulder level then pushes forwards palm facing forwards. Your right fist drops down beside your hip.

23a

23b

23c

23d

23e. Transfer your weight to your left leg. Turn your left palm up as your right fist crosses over the top of your left arm and strikes shoulder level, at the same time your left hand pulls back to the side of your hip, palm facing upwards.

23e   **Chop Back**

FORM 24 - STEP UP PARRY PUNCH

East

24a. Keeping your weight on your left leg, pull your right foot in on your toe. Your right hand drops down to your hip, fist facing upwards, your left hand lifts up to shoulder level, palm facing downwards, **(hold the ball).**

24b. Step through with your right leg onto your heel, your right palm turns into a fist and is supported at your wrist by your left hand, circle the hands forwards.

24c. Transfer your weight to your right leg, lift your left leg and step through onto your heel. Your left hand slides forwards, palm facing forwards, as your right fist pulls back towards your hip.

24d. Transfer your weight to your left leg and at the same time punch forwards with your right fist, your left palm stays where it is.

24a

24b

24c

24d

FORM 25 - STEP UP
GRASP THE BIRD'S TAIL

25a. Sit back and turn out your left foot 45°. Transfer your weight to your left leg and step up with your right leg. Your left hand raises to shoulder level palm facing downwards, as your right fist pulls into hip level, the fist opens, palm facing upwards, **(hold the ball).**

25b. Step away with your right foot and ward off, **(P'eng).** Your right palm is facing up and your left palm is facing down.

25a

25b

25c

25c. Turn your right palm down and your left palm up. Roll back **(Lu)** by dropping your left hand to your hip, whilst bringing your right hand into your shoulder, turning the palm inwards, as you transfer your weight to your left leg.

25d. & 25e. As your body weight is on your left leg, raise your left hand and place your palm onto your right wrist and then by pushing from your left leg, your weight is transferred to your right leg. Pressing, **(Ghi).**

25f. Your left hand slides over the top of your right hand, both palms facing downwards.

25g. Transfer your weight to your left leg and let your elbows drop slightly, (both palms are still facing downwards).

25d

25e

25f

25g

25h. By pushing from your left leg, transfer your body weight to your right leg, at the same time extend your arms slightly forwards, both palms facing forwards. Pushing, **(An).**

25h

FORM 26 - SINGLE WHIP

26a. Transfer your weight to your left leg to allow your right foot to turn inwards 45° on your heel. With palms facing downwards and arms held at shoulder level, rotate in an anti-clockwise circular motion.

26b. Drop your palms down to your hips (whilst carrying on with the circular motion), transfer your weight to your right leg. Raise your right hand to shoulder level and form a cranes beak, your left hand remains at your waist, palm facing upwards. At the same time pull in your left leg onto your toe.

26c. Step away with your left leg in the direction of West, your left hand turns outwards, palm facing West.

West

FORM 27 - CLOUD HANDS
(3,5 or 7 times)

27a. Circle your right hand clockwise so it becomes parallel with your left hand, both palms facing outwards and held at shoulder level. Transfer your weight to your right leg, (this allows you to turn your left foot inwards 45°). This is a transitional movement.
27b. By turning at your hips, both palms are pulling to your right (clockwise) until your right palm faces to your right and your left palm turns inwards to face your body. Even though your body is facing North, you are side stepping in the direction of West.

27a

27b

27c

27c. Transfer your weight to your left leg and place your right foot beside your left foot, toe then heel. Your left hand moves shoulder level to your left, (palm facing inwards) and your right hand circles downwards also to your left at hip level, (palm facing upwards). When you reach your left side, your left palm turns downwards, **(Hold the ball).**

27d. Now transfer your weight to your right leg and take a side step to your left with your left foot placing your toe down first, then your heel. Your right hand circles over to your right, (palm facing inwards), at shoulder level and your left hand circles downwards and to your right, (palm facing upwards), at hip level. When you reach your right, **hold the ball.**

27e. Now start to transfer your weight to your left leg whilst moving your hands to the left.

Please note that your left hand is circling anti-clockwise and your right hand is circling clockwise at all times.

27d

27e

27f

27f. Transfer your weight to your left leg and place your right foot beside your left foot, toe then heel. Your left hand moves shoulder level to your left, (palm facing inwards) and your right hand circles downwards also to your left at hip level, (palm facing upwards). When you reach your left side, your left palm turns downwards, **(Hold the ball).**

27g. Now transfer your weight to your right leg and take a side step to your left with your left foot placing your toe down first, then your heel. Your right hand circles over to your right, (palm facing inwards), at shoulder level and your left hand circles downwards and to your right, (palm facing upwards), at hip level. When you reach your right, **hold the ball.**

27h. Now start to transfer your weight to your left leg whilst moving your hands to your left.

Please note that your left hand is circling anti-clockwise and your right hand is circling clockwise at all times.

27g

27h

27i

27i. Transfer your weight to your left leg and place your right foot beside your left foot, toe then heel. Your left hand moves shoulder level to your left, (palm facing inwards) and your right hand circles downwards also to your left at hip level, (palm facing upwards). When you reach your left side, your left palm turns downwards, **(Hold the ball).**

112

FORM 28 - SINGLE WHIP

28a

28a. Your right hand circles out to your right (shoulder level), to form the cranes beak and your left hand circles downwards, then turns upwards, palm facing upwards at hip level, **(Hold the ball).** Your left foot raises up onto your toe.

28b. Step away with your left leg in the direction of West, your left hand turns outwards, palm facing West.

28b

113

FORM 29 - HIGH PAT ON HORSE

29a. Sit back and transfer your weight to your right leg. Both palms turn upwards held at shoulder level.

29b. As you start to rise upwards, your right arm bends at the elbow and your right palm moves in towards your right ear.

29c. Pull back your left palm into your hip (palm facing upwards), your right hand pushes forwards (palm facing down). Your left leg straightens so your left foot can lift up onto your toe.

FORM 30 - SEPARATE RIGHT FOOT

30a. Circle your right hand clockwise in towards your chest, your left hand raises to shoulder level. Lift up your left leg and step in the direction of South West.

30b. Continue to circle your right hand clockwise towards the direction of North West, turn the palm outwards. Place your left hand at your hip palm facing upwards.

30c. Your right hand circles underneath your left hand, both hands are now crossed at your wrists, both palms facing inwards and as you raise your palms to shoulder level, you raise your right knee at the same time. You then turn both palms outwards ready to kick.

30d. Separate your right foot (kick) North West. At the same time part your hands, your right palm circles to North West as you kick and your left hand circles back in the direction of South West. **When you separate right & left foot, you kick with your instep.**

30a

30b

30c

30d

FORM 31 - SEPARATE LEFT FOOT

31a. After the kick, place your right foot down in the direction of North West and circle your left hand anti-clockwise in towards your chest. Your right hand turns up and circles downwards (also anti-clockwise), towards your right side (hip).

31b. Continue to circle your left hand anti-clockwise towards the direction of South West, turn the palm outwards. Place your right hand at your hip palm facing upwards.

31c. Your left hand circles underneath your right hand, both hands are now crossed at your wrists, both palms facing inwards and as you raise your palms to shoulder level, you raise your left knee at the same time. You then turn both palms outwards ready to kick.

31d. Separate your left foot (kick) South West. At the same time part your hands, your left palm circles to South West and your right hand circles back in the direction of North West.

FORM 32 - TURN, KICK LEFT HEEL

32a. Without dropping your left leg, you pivot your right foot anti-clockwise so you are facing the direction of East. Your left leg stays bent (chambered), ready to kick. Your right and left wrists are crossed (shoulder level), palms facing inwards.

32b. Turn out both palms and kick with your left heel. At the same time part your hands, your left palm faces the same direction as the kick (East), and your right palm is turned outwards.

FORM 33 - BRUSH KNEE, PUSH
(2 times)

33a. Keeping your left leg bent (chambered), ready to step forwards onto your heel, your right palm turns upwards and drops to shoulder level and your left palm raises also to shoulder level and turns downwards.

33b. Step forwards onto your left heel, at the same time bend your right arm at the elbow bringing your right palm towards your right ear.

33c. As you transfer your weight to your left leg, your left hand sweeps across your left knee, palm facing downwards and your right palm pushes forwards.

33d. Sit back by putting your weight onto your right leg. This allows you to turn your left foot out 45°. Your right hand sweeps across to your left shoulder, palm facing downwards, your left palm just turns upwards at hip level, **(hold the ball).**

33e. Your right foot circles in towards your left foot as your left hand lifts up to your left shoulder (palm still facing upwards). Your right palm is still facing downwards.

33f. Place your right foot down heel first and as you transfer your weight to your right leg, your right hand sweeps across your right knee, palm facing downwards and your left palm pushes forwards.

FORM 34 - BRUSH KNEE, DOWNWARD PUNCH

34a. Your right hand drops down to your hip, palm facing upwards, as your left hand circles up to your right shoulder, palm facing down, **(hold the ball).**

34b. Your right hand rises up to shoulder level and forms a fist as your left leg steps forwards onto your heel.

34a

34b

34c

34c. Place your left toe down and at the same time your left hand sweeps across your left knee and your right fist punches downwards.

FORM 35 - TURN, SIDLE PUNCH

35a. Transfer your weight to your right leg and turn in your left foot 45°. Turning your hips to the direction of West, your right hand remains a fist and raises to hip level whilst your left hand raises up above your head, palm facing upwards.

35b. Pull in your right hand towards your body, raising it up towards your left shoulder. Your left hand circles down on the outside of your right arm to your left hip, at the same time you transfer your weight to your left leg and pull in your right foot onto your toe.

35c. Carrying on with the circular motion, your right fist pushes out to shoulder level as you step forwards with your right leg.

35d. Your left palm raises up the side of your body to shoulder level then pushes forwards palm facing forwards. Your right fist drops down beside your hip.

35a

35b

35c

35d

35e. Transfer your weight to your left leg. Turn your left palm up as your right fist crosses over the top of your left arm and strikes shoulder level, at the same time your left hand pulls back to the side of your hip, palm facing upwards.

35e   Chop Back

FORM 36 - STEP UP PARRY PUNCH

36a. Keeping your weight on your left leg, pull your right foot in on your toe. Your right hand drops down to your hip, fist facing upwards, your left hand lifts up to shoulder level, palm facing downwards, **(hold the ball).**

36b. Step through with your right leg onto your heel, your right palm turns into a fist and is supported at your wrist by your left hand, circle the hands forwards.

36c. Transfer your weight to your right leg, lift your left leg and step through onto your heel. Your left hand slides forwards, palm facing forwards, as your right fist pulls back towards your hip.

36d. Transfer your weight to your left leg and at the same time punch forwards with your right fist, your left palm stays where it is.

36a

36b

36c

36d

FORM 37 - KICK RIGHT HEEL

37a. Sit back and turn your left foot out 45°. Open your right palm and cross your hands, palms facing forwards, with your left hand on the inside.

37b. As you bend your left knee, circle both hands outwards and cross them once again by your left knee, palms facing upwards.

37c. Rise up onto your left leg. Your right leg is chambered and your hands are now crossed at shoulder level, palms facing inwards.

37d. Turn out and part both your palms and kick with the right heel. Your right palm is facing the same direction as your kick, (West) and your left palm turns outwards.

37a

37b

37c

37d

FORM 38 - HIT THE TIGER TO THE LEFT AND RIGHT

South East

38a. Place your right foot down beside your left foot and push both palms upwards.
38b. Circle both arms clockwise and once they reach shoulder level your left palm turns upwards and your right palm turns downwards. Lift up your left leg ready to step in the direction of South East.

38a

38b

38c   (Hit the Tiger to the left)

38c. Your left palm circles under your left knee and your right palm moves in to your hip. At this point both palms form fists and your left fist raises up above your head as you step out with your left leg, heel then toe, to the direction of South East.

HIT THE TIGER TO THE RIGHT

38d. Transfer your weight to your right leg, this will allow you to turn in your left foot 45°. Sit back onto your left leg and raise your right leg, ready to step in the direction of North West. Both fists turn back into open palms.

38e. Your right palm circles under your right knee and your left hand moves in to your hip. At this point both palms again form into fists and your right fist raises up above your head as you step out with your right leg, heel then toe, to the direction of North West.

126

FORM 39 - KICK RIGHT HEEL

39a. Turn your left foot out 45° and transfer your weight to your left leg. As you bend your left knee, circle both hands outwards and cross your palms, facing upwards.
39b. Rise up onto your left leg, your right leg is chambered. Your hands are now crossed at shoulder level palms facing inwards.

39a

39b

39c

39c. Turn out and part both your palms and kick with your right heel. Your right palm is facing the same direction as your kick, (west) and your left palm turns outwards.

FORM 40 - STRIKE OPPONENT WITH FISTS

40a. After your kick, chamber your right leg and pivot 45° on your left leg facing the direction of North West. Your left arm drops downwards (palm facing up), as your right palm turns upwards. Both palms rest beside your right knee.

40b. Step forwards placing your right foot down onto your heel. Circle both arms back to hip level. Continuing in a circular motion, both hands raise outwards to head level and form into fists as you transfer your weight forwards.

FORM 41 - KICK LEFT HEEL, TURN 360°

41a. Turn your right foot out 45° and transfer your weight to your right leg. As you bend your right knee open both fists, palms facing outwards, circle both hands downwards and cross your palms to face upwards.

41b. Rise up onto your right leg and lift your left leg. Your left leg is chambered and your hands are now crossed at shoulder level, palms facing inwards.

41c. Turn out and part both your palms and kick with your left heel. Your left palm is facing the same direction as your kick, (West) and your right palm turns outwards.

FORM 42 - KICK RIGHT HEEL

42a. Place your left leg down in the direction of East, (at this point both palms are held at shoulder level) and pivot on your right foot and turn your body 360° clockwise.

42b. You now transfer your weight to your left leg ready to chamber with your right leg. Both palms are now crossed facing inwards (your left palm is on the inside).

42c. Rise up onto your left leg, your right leg is chambered. Your hands are still crossed at shoulder level palms facing inwards.

42d. Turn out and part both your palms and kick with your right heel. Your right palm is facing the same direction as your kick, (West) and your left palm turns outwards.

42a

42b

42c

42d

FORM 43 - STEP UP PARRY PUNCH

43a. Your weight remains on your left leg as you lift your right leg, (chambered). Bring your left hand into your left shoulder, (palm facing downwards), your right hand moves to your hip (palm facing upwards) and forms a fist, **(hold the ball)**.

43b. Step through with your right leg onto your heel, your right fist is supported at your wrist by your left hand, circle both hands forwards.

43c

43c. Transfer your weight to your right leg, lift your left leg and step through onto your heel. Your left hand slides forwards, palm facing forwards, as your right fist pulls back towards your hip.

43d. Transfer your weight to your left leg and at the same time punch forwards with your right fist, your left palm stays where it is.

43d

FORM 44 - APPARENT CLOSE UP

44a. Your left hand slides under your right elbow. Your right fist opens, palm facing upwards.

44b. Your left hand slides up your right arm to the palm, both palms face upwards at shoulder level and open to shoulder width apart.

44c. Sit back transferring your weight to your right leg, drop your elbows slightly to turn your palms inwards to face each other.

44d. By pushing from your right leg, transfer your body weight to your left leg. At the same time push forwards with both palms.

FORM 45 - CROSS HANDS

45a. By turning at your hips, you transfer your body weight to your right leg. This allows you to turn your left foot in 45° on your heel. Your right hand is circling towards your right shoulder, your left hand stays where it is. The body is now facing towards the direction of North.

45a

45b. Transfer your body weight to your left leg and slide back your right foot so as they now become parallel. Both feet are shoulder width apart. At the same time both hands circle downwards and cross in front of the body, raising to shoulder level. Your left hand should be on the inside.

End of Section Two

45b

Yang Style Applications

of

SECTION 2

Bob Fermor performing Foo Kuin -Tiger Fist

Carry the Tiger to the Mountain

This is a counter to a roundhouse kick. As the kick comes in, block with your right hand and strike the attackers sternum with your left palm heel. Circle your right palm in, to strike the attackers face.

Fist Under Elbow

This is a counter to a punch. Parry the punch with your left palm while executing a left heel kick to the attackers right knee. Follow up with a right punch to the attackers floating ribs.

This is a counter to a punch. Parry the right punch with your left palm, grabbing the wrist. Step between the attackers legs, applying an elbow lock and push the attacker backwards.

Slant Flying

This is a counter to a punch. Parry the right punch with your outer right forearm, adhere to the attackers forearm. Step back with your right leg, pull the attacker down, whilst applying a wrist and elbow lock.

Needle at Sea Bottom

Flash Arm

This is a counter to a punch. Parry the right punch upwards with your right palm, step in with your left leg whilst executing a palm heel strike with your left hand to the attackers floating ribs.

Clouds Hands

This is a counter to a punch. Block the punch with your left palm, sweep your right hand under to apply a lock to the attackers elbow. Throw the attacker to your right by twisting your waist, whilst still applying pressure to the elbow.

This is a counter to a punch. Block the right punch downwards with your left palm, kick the attackers groin with your left instep and chop to the attackers throat with your right hand.

High Pat on Horse

This is a counter to a punch. Parry the punch with your right palm, grab the attackers arm and kick to the kidney area with your right foot. This kick can also be applied to the groin region.

Separate Right & Left Foot

This is a counter to a punch. Parry the punch with your right hand, grab the attackers wrist and execute a right heel kick to the floating ribs. This kick can also be applied to the solar plexus and sternum.

Kick Right & Left Heel

This is a follow up attack from kick right or left heel. After applying a heel kick, you follow up by striking the attacker with both your fists to the attackers temples, as you place down your foot.

Strike Opponent with Fists

Snake Creeps Down

Traditional Yang 85 Forms
SECTION 3
(Forms 46 through to 85)

Master Deng in Shanghai

FORM 46 - CARRY THE TIGER TO THE MOUNTAIN

46a. Transfer your weight to your right leg and turn your left foot inwards on your heel 45°. Drop your left hand down to your hip, palm facing upwards, right palm faces downwards, **(hold the ball).**

46b. Lift up your right leg and at the same time raise your left arm shoulder level. Right palm still faces downwards.

46c. Step to the direction of South East. Your right palm sweeps across your right knee, palm facing downwards and your left palm pushes forwards.

46d. Your right palm circles inwards towards your Dan Tien, palm still facing downwards.

46e. Your right palm continues circling upwards towards shoulder level, then turn your palm to face forwards.

46f. Turn your right palm down and your left palm up. Roll back **(Lu)** by dropping your left hand to your hip, whilst bringing your right hand into your shoulder, turning the palm inwards, as you transfer your weight to your left leg.

46g. & 46h. As your body weight is on your left leg, raise your left hand and place your palm onto your right wrist and then by pushing from your left leg, your weight is transferred to your right leg. Pressing, **(Ghi).**

46i. Your left hand slides over the top of your right hand and the hands open to shoulder width apart, both palms facing downwards.

46j. Transfer your weight to your left leg and drop your elbows slightly, (both palms are still facing downwards).

46k. By pushing from your left leg, transfer your body weight to your leading leg and at the same time turn both palms forwards and push. Pushing, **(An).**

46h

46i

46j

46k

FORM 47 - DIAGONAL SINGLE WHIP

47a. Transfer your weight to your left leg to allow your right foot to turn inwards 45° on your heel. With palms facing downwards and arms held at shoulder level, rotate in an anti-clockwise circular motion.

47b. Drop your palms down to your hips (whilst carrying on with the circular motion), transfer your weight to your right leg. Raise your right hand to shoulder level and form a cranes beak, your left hand remains at your waist, palm facing upwards. At the same time pull in your left leg onto your toe.

47a

47b

47c

47c. Step away with your left leg in the direction of North West, your left hand turns outwards, palm facing North West.

147

FORM 48 - PART THE WILD HORSES MANE (3 times)

48a. Circle your right hand clockwise, transfer your weight to your right leg and turn in your left foot 45°.

48b. Transfer your weight to your left leg and pull in your right leg on your toe. Your right hand circles down to your hip, open your hand, palm facing upwards and your left hand is held at shoulder level, palm facing downwards, **(hold the ball)**.

48c. Step away with your right leg in the direction of East and transfer your weight forwards. As your right arm moves to shoulder level, palm facing upwards, your left arm moves down to hip level, palm facing downwards.

48d. Sit back and turn out your right foot 45°. Now transfer your weight to your right leg. As your left foot steps up beside your right foot, your left hand circles across to your hip, palm facing upwards and your right hand pulls back to shoulder level, palm facing downwards, **(hold the ball).**

48e. Step away with your left leg in the direction of East and transfer your weight forwards. As your left arm moves to shoulder level, palm facing upwards, your right arm moves down to hip level, palm facing downwards.

48f

48f. Sit back and turn out your left foot 45°. Now transfer your weight to your left leg. As your right foot steps up beside your left foot, your right hand circles across to your hip, palm facing upwards, your left hand pulls back to shoulder level, palm facing downwards, **(hold the ball)**.

48g. Step away with your right leg in the direction of East and transfer your weight forwards. As your right arm moves to shoulder level, palm facing upwards, your left arm moves down to hip level, palm facing downwards.

48g

FORM 49 - STEP UP (Shoulder Stroke)
GRASP THE BIRD'S TAIL

49a. Transfer the weight to your right leg and place your left foot slightly in front of your right, formulating **(hold the ball)**.

49b. Your left foot steps out, (North). Rotate your hips to formulate shoulder stroke.

49c. Turn your hips, bring in your right foot while forming **(hold the ball)**.

49d. Step away with your right foot and ward off, **(P'eng)**.

49a

49b   (Shoulder Stroke)

49c

49d   (Ward Off - P'eng)

49e. Turn your right palm down and your left palm up. Roll back **(Lu)** by dropping your left hand to your hip, whilst bringing your right hand into your shoulder, turning the palm inwards, as you transfer your weight to your left leg.

49f. & 49g. As your body weight is on your left leg, raise your left hand and place your palm onto your right wrist and then by pushing from your left leg, your weight is transferred to your right leg. Pressing, **(Ghi).**

49h. Your left hand slides over the top of your right hand both palms facing downwards.

49e   (Roll Back- Lu)   49f   (Pressing - Ghi)

49g   49h

49i. Transfer your weight to your left leg, and let the elbows drop slightly, (both palms are still facing downwards).

49j. By pushing from your left leg, transfer your body weight to your right leg, at the same time extend your arms slightly forwards, both palms facing forwards. Pushing, **(An)**.

(Pushing - An)

FORM 50 - SINGLE WHIP

50a. Transfer your weight to your left leg to allow your right foot to turn inwards 45°
on your heel. With palms facing downwards and arms held at shoulder level, rotate in
an anti-clockwise circular motion.

50b. Drop your palms down to your hips (whilst carrying on with the circular motion),
transfer your weight to your right leg. Raise your right hand to shoulder level and form
a cranes beak, your left hand remains at your waist, palm facing upwards. At the same
time pull in your left leg onto your toe.

50a

50b

50c

50c. Step away with your left leg in the
direction of West, your left hand turns
outwards, palm facing West.

FORM 51 - FAIR LADY WORKS
THE SHUTTLES (to the 4 corners)

51a. Transfer your weight to your right leg and turn in your left foot 45°. Your left hand moves to your hip, palm facing upwards and your right hand opens up into a palm, held at shoulder level, palm facing downwards, **(hold the ball).**

51b. Transfer your weight to your left leg and pull in your right foot onto your toe. Turn your right palm to face inwards.

51c. & 51d. Step forwards with your right leg onto your heel, then step forwards with your left leg. At the same time raise your left arm above your head, turning your palm outwards and push your right palm forwards in the direction of North East, **(corner one).**

51a

51b

51c

51d   **corner one**

51e. Transfer your weight to your right leg and turn your left foot inwards 45°. Drop your left hand, palm facing inwards and place your right palm under your left elbow.

51f. Transfer your weight to your left leg and pull in your right foot onto your toe, step forwards with your right leg onto your heel, in the direction of North West.

51g. Transfer your weight to your right leg, At the same time raise your right arm above your head, turning your palm outwards and push your left palm forwards, **(corner two).**

51h. Step up with your left leg and place your left foot onto your toe beside your right foot. Drop your right arm palm facing inwards. Place your left hand underneath your right elbow, palm facing upwards.

51i. As you step forwards in the direction of South West, you transfer your weight to your left leg. At the same time raise your left arm above your head, turning your palm outwards and push your right palm forwards, **(corner three).**

corner three

51j. Transfer your weight to your right leg and turn your left foot inwards 45°. Drop your left hand, palm facing inwards and place your right palm under your left elbow.

51k. Transfer your weight to your left leg and pull in your right foot onto your toe, step forwards with your right leg onto your heel, in the direction of South East. As you step forwards and transfer your weight to your right leg raise your right arm above your head, turning your palm outwards and push your left palm forwards, **(corner four).**

corner four

FORM 52 - STEP UP (SHOULDER STROKE)
GRASP THE BIRD'S TAIL

52a. Your right foot turns inwards 45° and you place your left foot slightly in front of your right, formulating **(hold the ball)**.

52b. Your left foot steps out, (North). Rotate your hips to formulate shoulder stroke.

52c. Turn your hips, bring in your right foot while forming **(hold the ball)**.

52d. Step away with your right foot and ward off, **(P'eng)**

52a

52b   (Shoulder Stroke)

52c

52d   (Ward Off - P'eng)

52e. Turn your right palm down and your left palm up. Roll back **(Lu)** by dropping your left hand to your hip, whilst bringing your right hand into your shoulder, turning the palm inwards, as you transfer your weight to your left leg.

52f. & 52g. As your body weight is on your left leg, raise your left hand and place your palm onto your right wrist and then by pushing from your left leg, your weight is transferred to your right leg. Pressing, **(Ghi).**

52h. Your left hand slides over the top of your right hand both palms facing downwards.

52e   (Roll Back - Lu)   52f   (Pressing - Ghi)

52g   52h

52i. Transfer your weight to your left leg, and let the elbows drop slightly, (both palms are still facing downwards).

52j. By pushing from your left leg, transfer your body weight to your right leg, at the same time extend your arms slightly forwards, both palms facing forwards. Pushing, **(An).**

(Pushing - An)

FORM 53 - SINGLE WHIP

53a. Transfer your weight to your left leg to allow your right foot to turn inwards 45° on your heel. With palms facing downwards and arms held at shoulder level, rotate in an anti-clockwise circular motion.

53b. Drop your palms down to your hips (whilst carrying on with the circular motion), transfer your weight to your right leg. Raise your right hand to shoulder level and form a cranes beak, your left hand remains at your waist, palm facing upwards. At the same time pull in your left leg onto your toe.

53a

53b

53c

53c. Step away with your left leg in the direction of West, your left hand turns outwards, palm facing West.

FORM 54 - CLOUD HANDS
(3,5 or 7 times)

54a. Circle your right hand clockwise so it becomes parallel with your left hand, both palms facing outwards and held at shoulder level. Transfer your weight to your right leg, (this allows you to turn your left foot inwards 45°). This is a transitional movement.
54b. By turning at your hips, both palms are pulling to your right (clockwise) until your right palm faces to your right and your left palm turns inwards to face your body. Even though your body is facing North, you are side stepping in the direction of West.

54a

54b

54c

54c. Transfer your weight to your left leg and place your right foot beside your left foot, toe then heel. Your left hand moves shoulder level to your left, (palm facing inwards) and your right hand circles downwards also to your left at hip level, (palm facing upwards).

54d. Now transfer your weight to your right leg and take a side step to your left with your left foot placing your toe down first, then your heel. Your right hand circles over to your right, (palm facing inwards), at shoulder level and your left hand circles downwards and to your right, (palm facing upwards), at hip level. When you reach your right, **hold the ball.**

54e. Now start to transfer your weight to your left leg whilst moving your hands to the left.

Please note that your left hand is circling anti-clockwise and your right hand is circling clockwise at all times.

54f. Transfer your weight to your left leg and place your right foot beside your left foot, toe then heel. Your left hand moves shoulder level to your left, (palm facing inwards) and your right hand circles downwards also to your left at hip level, (palm facing upwards). When you reach your left side, your left palm turns downwards, **(Hold the ball).**

54g. Now transfer your weight to your right leg and take a side step to your left with your left foot placing your toe down first, then your heel. Your right hand circles over to your right, (palm facing inwards), at shoulder level and your left hand circles downwards and to your right, (palm facing upwards), at hip level. When you reach your right, **hold the ball.**

54h. Now start to transfer your weight to your left leg whilst moving your hands to your left.

Please note that your left hand is circling anti-clockwise and your right hand is circling clockwise at all times.

54g

54h

54i

54i. Transfer your weight to your left leg and place your right foot beside your left foot, toe then heel. Your left hand moves shoulder level to your left, (palm facing inwards) and your right hand circles downwards also to your left at hip level, (palm facing upwards). When you reach your left side, your left palm turns downwards, **(Hold the ball).**

FORM 55 - SINGLE WHIP

55a. Your right hand circles out to your right (shoulder level), to form the cranes beak and your left hand circles downwards, then turns upwards, palm facing upwards at hip level, **(Hold the ball).** Your left foot raises up onto your toe.

55b. Step away with your left leg in the direction of West, your left hand turns outwards, palm facing West.

FORM 56 - SNAKE CREEPS DOWN

56a. Turn out your right foot 45°, then bring in your left hand to your centre line, fingers pointing forwards. Sit back onto your right leg, ready to sweep along the ground and transfer your weight to your left leg. Your left palm leads the way.

56b. As your left palm sweeps forwards (West), close to the ground, start to turn out your left foot to the direction of West. You now start to transfer your weight to your left leg.

56c. As you start to rise up, turn your right foot inwards 45° on your heel. Your left palm pushes away to the direction of West and your right hand forms a cranes beak and circles behind your back at hip level, fingers pointing upwards.

FORM 57 - GOLDEN ROOSTER STANDS ON LEFT AND RIGHT LEGS

57a. & 57b. As you rise up into golden rooster, you will have to co-ordinate your in-breath and your out-breath, as it is a small and quick movement. As you rise up, you breathe in and as you hold the posture, you breathe out.

57a. Pull your right leg up and bend at your knee, (this will be your in-breath). Your left hand drops to hip level, palm facing downwards and your right hand opens (from cranes beak) and raises up to shoulder level, palm facing South. Your right leg stays chambered, toes pointing downwards.

57b. Take a side step to your right with your right leg in the direction of North, (this will be your in-breath). Place your right foot down and pull your left leg up and bend at your knee. Your right hand drops to hip level, palm facing downwards and your left hand raises up to shoulder level, palm facing North. Your left leg stays chambered, toes pointing downwards.

FORM 58 - REPULSE THE MONKEY
(3, 5 or 7 times)

58a. As your weight is on your right leg, your left leg steps backwards in the direction of East. You raise both palms upwards to shoulder level and as you step back with your left leg, bend your right arm at the elbow and bring in your right hand towards your face.

58b. By turning at your hips, transfer your weight to your left leg. Your left hand pulls back into your hip, palm facing upwards and your right hand pushes forwards, palm facing forwards. At the same time, turn in your right foot on the heel, so that your toe is facing forwards.

58c. All of your weight is on your left leg as you raise both palms upwards to shoulder level.

58d. As you step back with your right leg, bend your left arm at the elbow and bring in your left hand towards your face.

58e. By turning at your hips, transfer your weight to your right leg. Your right hand pulls back into your hip, palm facing upwards and your left hand pushes forwards, palm facing forwards. At the same time, turn in your left foot on the heel, so that your toe is facing forwards.

58f. All of your weight is on your right leg as you raise both palms upwards to shoulder level.

58g. As you step back with your left leg, bend your right arm at the elbow and bring in your right hand towards your face.

58f

58g

58h

58h. By turning at your hips, transfer your weight to your left leg. Your left hand pulls back into your hip, palm facing upwards and your right hand pushes forwards, palm facing forwards. At the same time, turn in your right foot on the heel, so that your toe is facing forwards.

FORM 59 - SLANT FLYING

59a. Your left hand raises up to shoulder level, palm facing down. Your right hand circles downwards to your hip, palm facing up. At the same time, your right foot pulls in, in front of your left foot, resting on your toe, **(hold the ball).**

59b. Step out on your heel in the direction of North East, with your right leg.

59a

59b

59c

59c. Transfer your weight to your right leg and stretch forwards with your right arm to shoulder level, palm facing upwards. Your left hand drops to your hip, palm facing downwards.

FORM 60 - RAISE HANDS

60a. Your left foot steps up behind your right foot and as you transfer your weight to your left leg, your right foot steps forwards onto your heel. Your right and left hands move into your centre line. Your left hand is now inline with your right elbow.

60a

FORM 61 - WHITE CRANE SPREADS ITS WINGS

61a. Pull back your right leg placing your foot onto your toe. Your right arm is formulating P'eng. Your left hand circles around to shoulder level.

61b. Your right leg steps forwards to the direction of North, allowing your body weight to transfer from your left to your right leg, at the same time your right arm drops, allowing you to apply shoulder stroke.

61a

61b

61c

61c. Now turn your body to the direction of West. Place your left foot onto your toe in front of your right foot. Your left palm is facing downwards and your right palm is facing upwards, **(hold the ball).**

61d. Your left hand drops down to hip level as you raise your right hand above your head to formulate White Crane.

61d

alternative angle

West

FORM 62 - BRUSH KNEE, PUSH

62a. Your right hand drops down to your hip, palm facing upwards. Your left hand circles up to your right shoulder, palm facing down, **(hold the ball).**

62b. Your right hand rises up to shoulder level as your left leg lifts up ready to step forwards onto your heel.

62c. Place your left foot down heel first and as you transfer your weight to your left leg, your left hand sweeps across your left knee, palm facing downwards and your right palm pushes forwards.

FORM 63 - NEEDLE AT SEA BOTTOM

West

63a. Step up with your right foot behind your left foot, transferring your weight to your right leg. Your left hand raises to touch your right wrist, both hands raise to shoulder level.

63b. Both hands circle in towards your chest, lifting up your left foot at the same time. You then place your left foot down onto your toe as your left hand sweeps across your left knee. The fingers of your right hand point directly down towards the floor.

FORM 64 - FLASH ARM

64a. Your left hand again touches your right wrist, raise both hands to shoulder level. As your body weight is still on your right leg, step forwards with your left leg and place your left foot down onto your heel.

64b. As you transfer your weight to your left leg, your right palm turns upwards and your arm raises above your head, at the same time your left palm pushes forwards.

178

FORM 65 - TURN, SIDLE PUNCH, SNAKE SHOWS ITS TONGUE

East

65a. Transfer your weight to your right leg and turn in your left foot 45°. Turning your hips to the direction of East, your right hand forms a fist and drops to hip level whilst your left hand raises up above your head, palm facing upwards.

65b. Pull in your right hand towards your body, raising it up towards your left shoulder. Your left hand circles down on the outside of your right arm to your left hip, at the same time you transfer your weight to your left leg and pull in your right foot onto your toe.

65c. Carrying on with the circular motion, you then open your right hand and push it out to shoulder level (palm facing inwards), as you step forwards with your right leg.

65d. Your left palm rises up the side of your body to shoulder level then pushes forwards palm facing forwards. Your right hand drops down beside your hip, (palm still open).

65a

65b

65c

65d

65e. Transfer your weight to your left leg. Turn your left palm up as your right hand forms back into a fist and crosses over the top of your left arm and strikes shoulder level, at the same time your left hand pulls back to the side of your hip, palm facing upwards.

65e   **Chop Back**

FORM 66 - STEP UP PARRY PUNCH

66a. Keeping your weight on your left leg, pull your right foot in on your toe. Your right hand drops down to your hip, fist facing upwards, your left hand lifts up to shoulder level, palm facing downwards, **(hold the ball).**

66b. Step through with your right leg onto your heel, your right palm turns into a fist and is supported at your wrist by your left hand, circle the hands forwards.

66c. Transfer your weight to your right leg, lift your left leg and step through onto your heel. Your left hand slides forwards, palm facing forwards, as your right fist pulls back towards your hip.

66d. Transfer your weight to your left leg and at the same time punch forwards with your right fist, your left palm stays where it is.

66a

66b

66c

66d

FORM 67 - STEP UP
GRASP THE BIRD'S TAIL

67a. Sit back and turn out your left foot 45°. Transfer your weight to your left leg and step up with your right leg. Your left hand raises to shoulder level palm facing downwards, as your right fist pulls into hip level, the fist opens, palm facing upwards, **(hold the ball).**

67b. Step away with your right foot and ward off, **(P'eng).** Your right palm is facing up and your left palm is facing down.

67a

67b

67c

67c. Turn your right palm down and your left palm up. Roll back **(Lu)** by dropping your left hand to your hip, whilst bringing your right hand into your shoulder, turning the palm inwards, as you transfer your weight to your left leg.

67d. & 67e. As your body weight is on your left leg, raise your left hand and place your palm onto your right wrist and then by pushing from your left leg, your weight is transferred to your right leg. Pressing, **(Ghi).**

67f. Your left hand slides over the top of your right hand, both palms facing downwards.

67g. Transfer your weight to your left leg and let your elbows drop slightly, (both palms are still facing downwards).

67h. By pushing from your left leg, transfer your body weight to your right leg, at the same time extend your arms slightly forwards, both palms facing forwards. Pushing, **(An).**

67h

FORM 68 - SINGLE WHIP

68a. Transfer your weight to your left leg to allow your right foot to turn inwards 45° on your heel. With palms facing downwards and arms held at shoulder level, rotate in an anti-clockwise circular motion.

68b. Drop your palms down to your hips (whilst carrying on with the circular motion), transfer your weight to your right leg. Raise your right hand to shoulder level and form a cranes beak, your left hand remains at your waist, palm facing upwards. At the same time pull in your left leg onto your toe.

68a

68b

68c

68c. Step away with your left leg in the direction of West, your left hand turns outwards, palm facing West.

185

FORM 69 - CLOUD HANDS
(3,5 or 7 times)

69a. Circle your right hand clockwise so it becomes parallel with your left hand, both palms facing outwards and held at shoulder level. Transfer your weight to your right leg, (this allows you to turn your left foot inwards 45°). This is a transitional movement.
69b. By turning at your hips, both palms are pulling to your right (clockwise) until your right palm faces to your right and your left palm turns inwards to face your body. Even though your body is facing North, you are side stepping in the direction of West.

69a

69b

69c

69c. Transfer your weight to your left leg and place your right foot beside your left foot, toe then heel. Your left hand moves shoulder level to your left, (palm facing inwards) and your right hand circles downwards also to your left at hip level, (palm facing upwards). When you reach your left side, your left palm turns downwards, **(Hold the ball).**

69d. Now transfer your weight to your right leg and take a side step to your left with your left foot placing your toe down first, then your heel. Your right hand circles over to your right, (palm facing inwards), at shoulder level and your left hand circles downwards and to your right, (palm facing upwards), at hip level. When you reach your right, **hold the ball.**

69e. Now start to transfer your weight to your left leg whilst moving your hands to the left.

Please note that your left hand is circling anti-clockwise and your right hand is circling clockwise at all times.

69d

69e

69f

69f. Transfer your weight to your left leg and place your right foot beside your left foot, toe then heel. Your left hand moves shoulder level to your left, (palm facing inwards) and your right hand circles downwards also to your left at hip level, (palm facing upwards). When you reach your left side, your left palm turns downwards, **(Hold the ball).**

69g. Now transfer your weight to your right leg and take a side step to your left with your left foot placing your toe down first, then your heel. Your right hand circles over to your right, (palm facing inwards), at shoulder level and your left hand circles downwards and to your right, (palm facing upwards), at hip level. When you reach your right, **hold the ball.**

69h. Now start to transfer your weight to your left leg whilst moving your hands to your left.

Please note that your left hand is circling anti-clockwise and your right hand is circling clockwise at all times.

69g

69h

69i

69i. Transfer your weight to your left leg and place your right foot beside your left foot, toe then heel. Your left hand moves shoulder level to your left, (palm facing inwards) and your right hand circles downwards also to your left at hip level, (palm facing upwards). When you reach your left side, your left palm turns downwards, *(*Hold the ball).**

FORM 70 - SINGLE WHIP

70a

70a. Your right hand circles out to your right (shoulder level), to form the cranes beak and your left hand circles downwards, then turns upwards, palm facing upwards at hip level, **(Hold the ball).** Your left foot raises up onto your toe.

70b. Step away with your left leg in the direction of West, your left hand turns outwards, palm facing West.

70b

FORM 71 - HIGH PAT ON HORSE

71a. Sit back and transfer your weight to your right leg. Both palms turn upwards held at shoulder level.

71b. As you start to rise upwards, your right arm bends at the elbow and your right palm moves in towards your right ear.

71a

71b

71c

71c. Pull back your left palm into your hip (palm facing upwards), your right hand pushes forwards (palm facing down). Your left leg straightens so your left foot can lift up onto your toe.

FORM 72 - FLOATING PALM

West

72a

72a. Raise your left leg and start to move your left hand forwards palm facing upwards, at the same time pull your right hand back towards your left elbow, palm facing downwards.

72b. As you pull back your right hand and move your left hand forwards, at the same time you take a step forwards with your left leg in the direction of west. Your left palm stays facing upwards, held at shoulder level and your right palm stays facing downwards held directly under your left elbow.

72b

FORM 73 - TURN, KICK RIGHT HEEL

73a. Transfer your weight to your right leg and turn in your left foot 45°. As your body turns, your right hand turns upwards and both hands cross, palms facing inwards and held at shoulder level.

73b. Rise up onto your left leg (your right leg is chambered), your hands are still crossed at shoulder level, palms facing inwards. As you start to kick, you then turn both palms outwards.

73a

73b

73c

73c. Turn out and part both your palms and kick with the right heel. Your right palm is facing the same direction as your kick, (East) and your left palm turns outwards.

FORM 74 - STEP UP PARRY DOWNWARD PUNCH

74a. Keeping your weight on your left leg, chamber your right leg. Your right hand drops down to your hip, palm facing upwards and forms into a fist, your left hand pulls into shoulder level, palm facing downwards, **(hold the ball).**

74b. Step through with your right leg onto your heel, your right fist is supported at your wrist by your left hand, circle the hands forwards.

74c. Transfer your weight to your right leg and lift your left leg. Your left hand slides forwards palm facing forwards and your right fist pulls back towards your hip.

74d. Your left leg now steps through and at the same time your left palm sweeps across your left knee, as your right fist punches downwards.

FORM 75 - STEP UP GRASP THE BIRD'S TAIL

75a. Sit back and turn out your left foot 45°. Transfer your weight to your left leg and step up with your right leg. Your left hand raises to shoulder level palm facing downwards, as your right fist pulls into hip level, the fist opens, palm facing upwards, **(hold the ball).**

75b. Step away with your right foot and ward off, **(P'eng).** Your right palm is facing up and your left palm is facing down.

75c. Turn your right palm down and your left palm up. Roll back **(Lu)** by dropping your left hand to your hip, whilst bringing your right hand into your shoulder, turning the palm inwards, as you transfer your weight to your left leg.

75a

75b

75c

75d

75d. & 75e. As your body weight is on your left leg, raise your left hand and place your palm onto your right wrist and then by pushing from your left leg, your weight is transferred to your right leg. Pressing, **(Ghi).**

75f. Your left hand slides over the top of your right hand, both palms facing downwards.

75g. Transfer your weight to your left leg and let your elbows drop slightly, (both palms are still facing downwards).

75h. By pushing from your left leg, transfer   your body weight to your right leg, at the same time extend your arms slightly forwards, both palms facing forwards. Pushing, **(An).**

75e

75f

75g

75h

FORM 76 - SINGLE WHIP

76a. Transfer your weight to your left leg to allow your right foot to turn inwards 45°
on your heel. With palms facing downwards and arms held at shoulder level, rotate in
an anti-clockwise circular motion.

76b. Drop your palms down to your hips (whilst carrying on with the circular motion),
transfer your weight to your right leg. Raise your right hand to shoulder level and form
a cranes beak, your left hand remains at your waist, palm facing upwards. At the same
time pull in your left leg onto your toe.

76a

76b

76c

76c. Step away with your left leg in the
direction of West, your left hand turns
outwards, palm facing West.

FORM 77 - SNAKE CREEPS DOWN

77a. Turn out your right foot 45°, then bring in your left hand to your centre line, fingers pointing forwards. Sit back onto your right leg, ready to sweep along the ground and transfer your weight to your left leg. Your left palm leads the way.

77b. As your left palm sweeps forwards (West), close to the ground, start to turn out your left foot to the direction of West. You now start to transfer your weight to your left leg.

77a

77b

77c

77c. As you start to rise up, turn your right foot inwards 45° on your heel. Your left palm pushes away to the direction of West and your right hand forms a cranes beak and circles behind your back at hip level, fingers pointing upwards.

FORM 78 - FORM THE SEVEN STARS

78a. Keeping your weight on your left leg, turn your left foot outwards 45°. Your left hand drops down beside your hip, your right hand opens and drops parallel with your left hand, palms facing backwards.

78b. Step through with your right foot, placing the foot onto your toe. At the same time both hands raise up the side of your body towards your armpits and form fists. You then push your arms forwards at shoulder level and cross the fists, at the wrists (right under left).

FORM 79 - RETREAT TO RIDE THE TIGER

79a

79a. Take a step backwards with your right foot (East) and place your left foot onto your toes in front of your right foot. Open your palms and turn your right palm upwards and drop it to your hip. Your left palm stays facing downwards, **(hold the ball).**

79b. Your left hand sweeps down clockwise, across to your left hip and your right hand raises up above your head (palm facing upwards), to formulate 'Retreat to Ride the Tiger'.

79b

FORM 80 - TURN, WHITE LOTUS KICK

80a. Circle your left hand above your head clockwise as your right hand circles in to your shoulder also clockwise, (palm facing downwards). Your legs remain in the same position.

80b. You now raise up onto your toes and pivot clockwise. You turn to the direction of South West. Your right palm faces outwards South West, your left hand drops to hip level, palm facing downwards.

80c. Your left foot now steps in the direction of South.

80d. Chamber your right leg and turn both palms to face downwards at shoulder level.

80e. Start to swing your right leg upwards in a clockwise motion. As you swing your leg, you kick both hands, your left palm first and then your right palm.

(This kick should be executed as you would apply an Outer Crescent Kick).

80e

West

FORM 81 - ARCHER SHOOTING
THE TIGER

81a. After your kick, place your right foot down in the direction of West, onto your heel. Turn your right palm up and keep your left palm down and circle both palms downwards towards your right knee.

81b. As you start to transfer your weight to your right leg, both palms start to raise upwards towards your shoulder again.

81a

81b

81c

81c. As your weight is moving forwards to your right leg, you form a fist with both hands and pull back with your right fist, stopping at eyebrow level. At the same time you punch forwards with your left fist in the direction of West.

FORM 82 - STEP UP PARRY PUNCH

82a. Transfer the weight to your left leg as you lift your right leg, (chambered). Open your left palm and bring it across to your left shoulder, (palm facing downwards), your right hand moves to hip level (palm facing upwards) still forming a fist, **(hold the ball)**.
82b. Step through with your right leg onto your heel, your right fist is supported at your wrist by your left hand, circle both hands forwards.
82c. Transfer your weight to your right leg, lift your left leg and step through onto your heel. Your left hand slides forwards, palm facing forwards, as your right fist pulls back towards your hip.
82d. Transfer your weight to your left leg and at the same time punch forwards with your right fist, your left palm stays where it is.

FORM 83 - APPARENT CLOSE UP

83a. Your left hand slides under your right elbow. Your right fist opens, palm facing upwards.

83b. Your left hand slides up your right arm to the palm, both palms face upwards at shoulder level and open to shoulder width apart.

83c. Sit back transferring your weight to your right leg, drop your elbows slightly to turn your palms inwards to face each other.

83d. By pushing from your right leg, transfer your body weight to your left leg. At the same time push forwards with both palms.

83a

83b

83c

83d

FORM 84 - CROSS HANDS

84a

84a. By turning at your hips, you transfer your body weight to your right leg. This allows you to turn your left foot in 45° on your heel. Your right hand is circling towards your right shoulder, your left hand stays where it is. The body is now facing towards the direction of North.

84b. Transfer your body weight to your left leg and slide back your right foot so as they now become parallel. Both feet are shoulder width apart. At the same time both hands circle downwards and cross in front of the body, raising to shoulder level. Your left hand should be on the inside.

End of Section Three

84b

FORM 85 - CLOSING FORM

85a. Leaving your feet where they are, turn both your palms downwards and stretch out both arms at shoulder level. Open up your arms, shoulder width apart.

85b. Bend your elbows and drop them towards your hips as you bend your knees. As your body is sinking you transfer your weight to your right leg, this will allow you to step in with your left foot and place it down beside your right foot.

85c. As you place down your left foot, you now take another side step with your right foot placing it down shoulder width apart. Your hands are held loosely at your sides, palms facing south.

This is the end of the 85 Forms

85c

Yang Style Applications

of

SECTION 3

Bob Fermor peforming Tiger Claw from Foo Kuin, Tiger Fist

Part the Wild Horses Mane

Parry the left punch with your left palm, grab on and step behind the attacker with your right leg. Come underneath with your right arm and throw the attacker back by applying pressure across the chest.

This is a counter to a punch. Block the left punch upwards with your right arm whilst executing a palm heel strike with your left palm under the attackers chin.

Fair Lady Works the Shuttles

This is a counter to a punch. Block the left punch upwards with your right palm, grab on and step in striking to the groin with a left ridge hand, then throw the attacker over your shoulder.

Snake Creeps Down

This is a counter to a hook punch. Duck under the left hook and grasp the attacker behind the neck with your left hand. Pull the attacker on as you execute a left knee to the sternum followed by a kick to the groin with your left instep.

Golden Rooster Stands on Left & Right Leg

This is a counter to a punch. Parry the right punch downwards with your left palm, and then strike with the back of your right hand to the attackers face.

Snake Shows its Tongue

This is a counter to a punch. Parry the right punch downwards with your right palm, as you strike to the attackers throat with the fingers of your left hand, palm facing upwards, and then kick to the groin with your left instep.

Floating Palm

Form the Seven Stars

This is a counter to a punch. Apply a cross block to the right punch and parry punch over to your right with your right palm then kick to the attackers groin with your right instep.

Retreat to Ride the Tiger

This is a counter to two punches. Block the left punch upwards with your right hand. The Attacker then throws a right punch, block this downwards with your left palm and kick to the attackers groin with your left instep.

This is a counter to a punch. Block the right punch with your right hand and grab hold. Pull the attackers right arm down and kick the attacker to the face with an outer crescent kick.

White Lotus Kick

This is a counter to a punch. Block the left punch outwards with your right forearm whilst punching to the attackers sternum or solar plexus with your left fist.

Archer Shooting the Tiger

Bob Fermor demonstrating Dat-Mo Cane

Joanne Fermor playing Lion Dance

Yang - Style
Single Hand
Tui Sau (exercises)

Master Deng demonstrating Pushing Hands

Master Deng
Once made a quote, he said
"To defeat your opponent you must first become one".

PUSHING HANDS

When I began learning Tai Chi from Master Deng, he insisted that we put as much time and effort into Pushing Hands training as we did into the Tai Chi form. He wanted to make it clear that when practising Pushing Hands, there should be no aggressive action towards one another and it was certainly no place for egos. Pushing Hands exercise is where two people train together. They learn to feel by utilising one's 'listening energy' and 'adhere', which is to use one's 'sticking energy'.

Master Deng once made a quote, he said, 'to defeat your opponent you must first become one'. To achieve this you must work together in harmony.

What is the point behind Pushing Hands? There are two objectives, firstly to avoid an attack and secondly to penetrate one's defence. There are many drills practised in Pushing Hands and it will normally begin with Single Pushing Hands. This exercise is normally carried out by two people standing opposite each other. The correct positioning of the feet is as follows: both partner's left feet are placed close together side by side with a foot length gap between them **(see photo A)**, then both partner's right feet step back shoulder width apart, into a natural ready position. The body weight is distributed equally on both legs, (central equilibrium), **(see photo B)**.

The left hand is then placed behind the back of the body. It is here when you should decide with your partner who is going to be the attacker and who is going to be the defender. Once this has been decided, both partner's right hands raise up to shoulder level, connected at the back of the wrists, elbows dropped.

EXERCISE ONE: Single Pushing Hands - **Attack the sternum**

Once you have decided who is going to start the exercise, the attacker initiates the attack by pushing towards their partner's centre line. Transferring all their body weight to their leading leg, then turning their hand so as their palm is pushing against the back of the defender's hand, (this also pushes the defender's body weight to their rear leg), the defender creates a space between their hand and body, this is called 'P'eng'. They turn their waist clockwise simultaneously grasping the attacker's wrist, this in turn puts the defender's palm onto the back of the attacker's hand. Now the defender becomes the attacker, exercise complete. **Just repeat the exercise as many times as you like.**

EXERCISE TWO: Single Pushing Hands
Attack Dan Tien & face

On this exercise, the attacker changes direction, by pushing towards the defender's Dan Tien and transferring their body weight to the leading leg, (remember the palm is pushing against the back of the defender's hand). This now pushes the defender's body weight to their rear leg. The defender turns their hand simultaneously grasping the attacker's wrist, this puts the defender's palm onto the back of the attacker's hand. Now the defender becomes the attacker and counter attacks by pushing their hand towards the attacker's face, exercise complete. **Just repeat the exercise as many times as you like.**

EXERCISE THREE: Single Pushing Hands
Attacking the heart

Once again the attacker changes direction, by lifting up their elbow and pushing towards the defender's heart, putting all their body weight to their leading leg (remember the palm is pushing against the back of the defender's hand). This pushes the defender's body weight to their rear leg.   The defender turns their hand simultaneously grasping the attacker's wrist. Now the defender becomes the attacker and counter attacks by lifting up their elbow and pushing towards the attacker's heart, exercise complete. **Just repeat the exercise as many times as you like.**

Points to remember on the first three exercises

1: When you grasp your partner's wrist on the defence, remember your body weight is on your back leg. Don't pull them directly towards you, as they will knock you off balance. Think of a compass, if you are facing North and the attacker is facing South, when you turn your hips to the right, you will re-direct your attacker's energy or force South East, resulting in the attacker being vulnerable. Once their energy or force is deflected in that direction, it is at this point where you can defeat your partner very easily by just 'firing' them out.

2: You must make sure that you are tucking at all times and you must remain loose at the waist during the Pushing Hand exercises. This will enable you to have a strong root and posture at all times.

3: You must try to stay relaxed at all times, there should be no tension within the arms or body. It is only when this is administered that you can start to utilise your 'listening energy'. To utilise this 'listening energy' is to know and sense when your partner is going to launch their next attack. You can feel this within their body movement. It is like a boxer when they throw a punch their shoulder moves first.

4: 'Adhere' or 'sticking energy'. This is applied by learning to stick to your partner. Where your partner goes, you follow them, always adhering. Learning to stick to your partner will help you to shut your opponent down in any possible attack. Master Deng once quoted   **'if your opponent is quick, you are quick, if he is slow you are slow'.**

TUI SAU - SINGLE PUSHING HAND EXERCISE
Exercise 1 - strike sternum

TUI SAU - SINGLE PUSHING HAND EXERCISE
Exercise 2 - strike Dan Tien & face

TUI SAU - SINGLE PUSHING HAND EXERCISE
Exercise 3 - strike the heart

TUI SAU - Exercise 4 - lock on elbow

From this exercise onwards we start to utilise both hands. In this exercise one hand is adhering to your opponent's wrist, whilst the other hand incorporates a locking technique to your partners elbow.

TUI SAU - Exercise 5 - lock on elbow & shoulder

This exercise is similar to exercise 4. The difference is, instead of applying an elbow lock with your forearm, you apply an elbow lock with your open palm, allowing you to apply a shoulder lock at the same time. Again the other hand is adhering to your opponent's wrist.

TUI SAU - Exercise 6 - silk reeling (free-style Tui Sau)

Silk reeling is a very basic Pushing Hand exercise. It is very useful to bring students on in their training, as it allows them to adhere and to push their opponent straight away, but it is not a practical exercise for applying locks, throws or sweeps. 'Grasping the Bird's Tail' is far more practical for these types of applications.

It is important to note that both hands of both practitioners are circling inwards at all times.

Bob & Joanne - Foo Kuin Tiger Fist

Yang - Style
Double Hand
Tui Sau (exercises)

Master Deng in Shanghai

**Master Deng once made a quote, he said
"the applications should be applied in the same way
as they are visually performed within the practise of the 85 Forms".**

GRASP THE BIRD'S TAIL

'Grasp the Bird's Tail' is undoubtedly the most important form in the Yang Style 85 Forms. It is repeated 8 times (including the interpretation of 'Carry the Tiger to the Mountain'). In Pushing Hands, 'Grasp the Bird's Tail' is the linking form to the other sequences. Whenever you incorporate a different routine like 'Part the Wild Horses Mane', 'Single Whip' or 'Cloud Hands', they are all linked to 'P'eng', 'Lu', 'Ghi', 'An'. All the changes are normally intercepted from 'Ghi' (pressing) or 'P`eng' (ward off). From 'Ghi' or 'P`eng', you can also change direction whether it be clockwise or anti-clockwise.

If you are practising 'Grasp the Bird's Tail' and you want to 'fire' or 'Far Ging' your opponent out with, for example: 'Cloud Hands' and if your opponent feels your intentions, he will automatically 'ward off' and revert back to 'Grasp the Bird's Tail'. This not only makes 'Grasp the Bird's Tail' the most important move, but also the main linking move to the applications of all the forms.

It is important to note that Pushing Hands training consists of counter upon counter, just like Judo. 'Grasp the Bird's Tail' and all the other routines ('Single Whip', 'Cloud Hands', 'Brush Knee Push' etc.), have there own individual Tui Sau routine. I have met many Tai Chi practitioners that believe that the Grasp the Bird's Tail Tui Sau routine, is all that is needed to perfect their sensitivity skills. I myself feel that this cannot be true as Yang Lu Chan would have said, just repeat Grasp the Bird's Tail 85 times and forget the rest. Master Deng always insisted that you have to incorporate the other techniques to make Yang Style a complete martial art system, could you imagine a martial art system without a kick, I don't think so!

Grasp the Bird's Tail - Applications

Dave attacks with a right snap punch, Joanne counter attacks with Ward Off (P'eng).

Dave attacks with a left reverse punch to the body, Joanne counter attacks with Roll Back (Lu).

3

Joanne then delivers pressing which traps Dave's left arm (Ghi).

4

Dave counter attacks by rotating his hips and strikes Joanne with his fists. Joanne intercepts Dave's elbows stopping the attack.

5

Joanne counter attacks by Pushing down on Dave's arms.

6

Joanne then delivers a double palm push to Dave's chest (An).

You will see from this section that Pushing Hands sensitivity training is much more than simply 'Grasp the Bird's Tail'. All of the 37 postures that make the 85 forms can be incorporated into the routines, as taught traditionally by the true masters of Tai Chi such as, Yang Lu Chan, Yang Cheng Fu and Master Deng.

TUI SAU - DOUBLE PUSHING HAND EXERCISE
Exercise 7 - Grasp the Bird's Tail

P'eng
(ward off)

Bob applies (clockwise)

Lu
(roll back)

Please note: Adhere to your partner at all times and always stay relaxed. The following photographs are purely for reference only and to give you some idea of how to play each exercise. Master Deng always said **'a book is only a reference, not a teacher'**.

Ghi
(pressing)

Note: It is not easy to learn something as complex as pushing hands from a sequence of pictures. This is why it is important to learn from a good teacher, but however, it will surely wet your appetite.

An
(push)

Grasp the Bird's Tail
Joanne applies (anti-clockwise)

P'eng

Lu

Ghi

An

Grasp the Bird's Tail
Bob applies (anti-clockwise)

P'eng

Lu

TUI SAU - DOUBLE PUSHING HAND EXERCISE
Exercise 8 - Opening Form

Joanne applies double palms to Bob's shoulders.

Bob adheres and deflects double palms by raising elbows.

Bob counter attacks by applying double palms to Joanne's shoulders.

TUI SAU - DOUBLE PUSHING HAND EXERCISE
Exercise 9 - Part the Wild Horses Mane

1: Bob and Ali both ward off.

2: Bob steps back with left leg.

3: Bob applies Part the Wild Horses Mane.

4: Ali steps back left leg.

5: Both ward off.

6: Ali steps back right leg.

7: Ali applies Part the Wild Horses Mane.

8: Bob steps back right leg.

To keep within the boundaries of the Yang Style Tai Chi, Master Deng once told me, 'when you learn Tai Chi there are rules and once you have mastered Tai Chi there are no rules'. It is plain to see what is being interpreted when playing the Yang 85 Forms. It is not acceptable to have many different applications that are non-applicable to the actual technique that is being performed within the Yang 85 Forms.

Bob and Ali both ward off

9

TUI SAU - DOUBLE PUSHING HAND EXERCISE
Exercise 10 - White Crane Spreads it's Wings

1: Bob and Ali both ward off.

2: Bob rolls back, Ali applies pressing.

3: Bob intercepts and applies White Crane.

4: Ali counter attacks by drawing in his left arm.

5: Ali draws Bob into pressing.

6: Bob and Ali both ward off.

TUI SAU - DOUBLE PUSHING HAND EXERCISE
Exercise 11 - Single Whip

1:Bob and Ali both ward off.

2: Bob rolls back, hooks on with left cranes beak.

3: Bob applies Single Whip.

4: Ali circles out left hand.

5: Bob rolls back draws Ali into pressing.

6: Bob and Ali both ward off.

TUI SAU - DOUBLE PUSHING HAND EXERCISE
Exercise 12 - Brush Knee, Push

Brush knee push action shot.

1: Bob and Ali both ward off.

2: Ali rolls back, Bob applies Brush Knee Push.

3: Ali counters by guiding Bob's left elbow.

4: Ali circles anti-clockwise

5: Bob double palms Ali into pressing.

6: Bob and Ali both ward off.

7: Bob rolls back, Ali applies Brush Knee Push.

8: Bob counters by guiding Ali's left elbow.

9: Bob circles clockwise.

10: Ali double palms Bob into pressing.

11: Bob and Ali both ward off.

TUI SAU - DOUBLE PUSHING HAND EXERCISE
Exercise 13 - Cloud Hands

Cloud Hands action shot.

1: Bob and Ali both ward off.

2: Ali rolls back.

3: Bob applies pressing.

4: Ali pushes Bob's left shoulder, Bob
counter attacks by applying Cloud Hands.

5: Bob circles Ali's right arm anti-clockwise.

6: Ali double palms Bob into pressing.

7:Bob pushes left shoulder, Ali uses Cloud Hands.

8: Ali circles Bob's right arm anti-clockwise.

9: Bob double palms Ali into pressing.

10: Ali circles upwards.

11: Bob and Ali both ward off.

TUI SAU - DOUBLE PUSHING HAND EXERCISE
Exercise 14 - Repulse the Monkey

Repulse the Monkey action shot.

1: Bob and Ali both ward off.

2: Bob applies Repulse the Monkey.

3: Ali steps back with left leg & pulls Bob on.

4: Bob steps in with right leg.

5: Bob rolls back.

6: Bob and Ali both ward off.

7: Ali applies Repulse the Monkey.

8: Bob steps back with right leg & pulls Ali on.

9: Ali steps in with right leg.

10: Ali rolls back.

11: Bob and Ali both ward off.

TUI SAU - DOUBLE PUSHING HAND EXERCISE
Exercise 15 - Hit the Tiger

Double palm push action shot.

1: Bob and Ali both ward off.

2: Ali rolls back.

3: Bob applies pressing.

4: Bob circles left fist outside to apply Hit the Tiger.

5: Ali circles Bob's arm clockwise.

6: Bob rolls back.

7: Ali applies pressing.

8: Ali circles left fist outside applys Hit the Tiger.

9: Bob circles Ali's arm clockwise.

10: Bob rolls back.

11: Bob and Ali both ward off.

TUI SAU - DOUBLE PUSHING HAND EXERCISE
Exercise 16 - High Pat on Horse

1: Bob and Ali both ward off.

2: Bob applies High Pat on Horse, left chop.

3: Bob applies High Pat on Horse, right chop.

4: Ali applies High Pat on Horse, left chop.

5: Ali applies High Pat on Horse, right chop.

6: Bob and Ali both ward off.

TUI SAU - DOUBLE PUSHING HAND **EXERCISE**
Exercise 17 - Fair Lady Weaves the Shuttles

1: Bob and Ali both ward off.

2: Bob intercepts with right arm.

3: Bob applies Fair Lady.

4: Ali drops right elbow circling anti-clockwise.

5: Bob rolls back.

6: Ali applies pressing.

TUI SAU - DOUBLE PUSHING HAND EXERCISE
Exercise 18 - Golden Rooster Stands on Both Legs

Golden Rooster action shot.

1: Bob and Ali both ward off.

2: Ali rolls back.

3: Bob applies pressing.

4: Bob's right hand grabs behind Ali's neck.

5: Bob applies Golden Rooster right side.

6: Ali counters by stepping back, Bob presses.

7: Bob's left hand grabs behind Ali's neck.

8: Bob applies Golden Rooster left side.

9: Ali counters by stepping back and rolls back.

10: Bob applies pressing.

11: Bob and Ali both ward off.

TUI SAU - DOUBLE PUSHING HAND **EXERCISE**
Exercise 19 - Separate Right & Left Foot

1: Bob and Ali both ward off.

2: Bob applies pressing.

3: Bob sits back and chambers left leg.

4: Bob applies Separate left foot.

5: Ali steps back and rolls back.

6: Bob applies pressing.

7: Bob sits back and chambers right leg.

8: Bob applies Separate right foot.

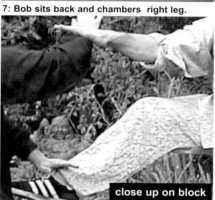

close up on block

9: Ali steps back and rolls back.

10: Bob applies pressing.

11: Bob and Ali both ward off.

TUI SAU - DOUBLE PUSHING HAND EXERCISE
Exercise 20 - Turn & Sidle Punch

1: Bob and Ali both ward off.

2: Bob rolls back.

3: Bob circles left fist inside applying Sidle Punch.

4: Ali rolls back.

5: Ali circles right fist inside applying Sidle Punch.

6: Bob and Ali both ward off.

TUI SAU - DOUBLE PUSHING HAND EXERCISE
Exercise 21 - Raise Hands

1: Bob and Ali both ward off.

2: Bob applies Raise Hands.

3: Ali rolls back.

4: Ali applies Raise Hands.

5: Bob rolls back.

6: Bob and Ali both ward off.

TUI SAU - DOUBLE PUSHING HAND EXERCISE
Exercise 22 - Strike Opponent with Fists

Strike Opponent with Fists action shot.

1: Bob and Ali both ward off.

2: Bob applies pressing.

3: Bob circles both hands outwards.

4: Bob applies Strike Opponent with Fists.

5: Ali circles Bob's right arm anti-clockwise.

6: Ali applies pressing.

7: Ali circles both hands outwards.

8: Ali applies Strike Opponent with Fists.

9: Bob circles Ali's left arm anti-clockwise.

10: Bob applies pressing.

11: Bob and Ali both ward off.

TUI SAU - DOUBLE PUSHING HAND **EXERCISE**
Exercise 23 - Snake Creeps Down

Snake Creeps Down action shot.

1: Bob and Ali both ward off.

2: Ali rolls back.

3: Bob applies pressing.

4: Bob drops left shoulder.

5: Bob applies Snake Creeps Down.

6: Bob and Ali both ward off.

7: Bob rolls back.

8: Ali applies pressing.

9: Ali drops left shoulder.

10: Ali applies Snake Creeps Down.

11: Bob and Ali both ward off.

像掛生先甲元霍

Bob Fermor, Mr Chang & Mr Wong at the Chin Woo Athletic Association, Shanghai, China

Yang - Style
Walking Pushing Hands
Tui Sau (exercises)

Bob and Joanne walking the circle

TUI SAU - MOVING PUSHING HANDS
Exercise 1

In this exercise you are playing Grasp the Bird's Tail only. The object of this exercise is to incorporate foot movement. When Bob raises his left leg, Joanne raises her right leg and when Bob raises his right leg, Joanne raises her left leg. It is important to co-ordinate your footwork with your hand movement.

TUI SAU - MOVING PUSHING HANDS
Exercise 2 - Three step

Still incorporating Grasp the Bird's Tail, it is now time to start taking three steps backwards and three steps forwards.

It is important to note: As you step backwards and forwards, you incorporate P'eng, Lu, Ghi, An. The timing on this exercise is very important.

Bob is taking the lead. He initiates the first movement by taking a step backwards.

1: Bob and Joanne both ward off.

2: Bob steps back, applies roll back.

3: It is important to note that during the roll back, the hands are moving slower than the footwork.

4: Bob is pushing & Joanne is pressing.

5: Bob and Joanne both ward off.

6: Joanne steps back, applies roll back.

7: Joanne is pushing & Bob is pressing.

Please note: After photo 7, both return to ward off. Repeat as many times as you like.

TUI SAU - MOVING PUSHING HANDS
Exercises 3 - 180° turn

1: Bob and Joanne both ward off .

2: Joanne steps around Bob's right leg.

3: Bob rolls back as Joanne steps around with her left leg. Bob also takes a step with his left. As they both raise their right legs, they square off.

4: Bob is pushing & Joanne is pressing.

5: Bob and Joanne both ward off.

TUI SAU - MOVING PUSHING HANDS
Exercises 4 - walk the circle

In this exercise, when you walk the circle you lead with your right hand. The back of the wrists adhere at all times, whilst the left hand is held at hip level. You are performing ward off on the circle.

change direction

**Ben, Joanne, Bob,
Jordan & Brandon.**

The Fermor clan

DA-LU
THE EIGHT CO-ORDINAL DIRECTIONS

In Da-Lu, you learn to incorporate your elbow and shoulder as you walk the eight trigram circle, known as the eight co-ordinal directions. You adhere at the wrist and elbow, when facing each other at the four points and utilise your shoulder stroke at the four corners.

Directions of Da-lu

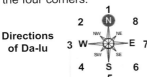

1: Bob and Joanne both ward off.

2: Bob & Joanne both step out with left leg.

3: Joanne applies shoulder stroke.

4: Bob & Joanne both step out with left leg.

5: Bob and Joanne both ward off.

6: Bob & Joanne both step out with left leg.

7: Bob applies shoulder stroke.

8: Bob & Joanne both step out with left leg.

9: Bob and Joanne both ward off.

10: Bob & Joanne both step out with left leg.

11: Joanne applies shoulder stroke.

12: Bob & Joanne both step out with left leg.

13: Bob and Joanne both ward off.

14: Bob & Joanne both step out with left leg.

15: Bob applies shoulder stroke.

16: Bob & Joanne both step out with left leg.

17: Bob and Joanne both ward off.

PLATFORM FOR PUSHING HANDS TRAINING

1: Bob & Dave both ward off on platform.

2: Bob & Dave play pushing hands on the platform, both blindfolded. Bob applies Repulse the Monkey.

The platform is perfect for training your balance and to add a new level to your training.

The dimensions of the platform are as follows:

>**Width 2 foot, 6 inches,**
>**Length 7 foot long,**
>**The height is up to you.**

When training on the platform, always be careful and have some students standing around the platform just in case someone falls awkwardly.

CONCLUSION

This book was never designed to replace a teacher, it is purely to wet one's appetite in the true traditional art of Tai Chi Chuan. Having trained under Master Deng Er Qian, I look at martial arts in a different light. Whenever I see an art performed, I always want to know in-depth what each movement is for, specifically the martial art content. I have never stopped being amazed and impressed by some of the masters that I have come across on my travels around the world. I will always practise traditional Yang Style Tai Chi Chuan the way it was taught to me by Master Deng Er Qian.

Bob and Joanne's other passion in their lives is their German Shepherds.

You can find out further information about the
National Academy of Martial Arts
by visiting the official website at:

WWW.NAMA.CO.UK

Michael Alexander Gordon

June 26th 1974 - May 23rd 2001

Michael will be sadly missed by us all. To die at such a young age is a tragedy and will be difficult to come to terms with.

He was a dedicated student of the martial arts for many years. He was always a happy lad and always keen to do well. He was a sensitive and kind hearted person and he idolised his mother and father, Mary and Michael very much. He was much loved by his uncle Lenny and his aunt Sylvia and the rest of his family.

Michael had a son and a daughter, Tyler and Chanesse, who will miss their father very much. We hope through them Michael's spirit will live on.

God bless you Michael, you have made your mark on earth my son and that is, within our hearts you will never be forgotten. We all hope that one day our paths will cross once again, maybe in another life.
God bless.

Bob and Joanne Fermor.